T0198779

KUBLAI KHAN

(COMPLETED ... OF UNFINISHED COLERIDGE)

TARIQ HAMEED

WHEN DONE'S DONE, THEN DONE 'TWERE 'NER UNDONE

AuthorHouse™ UK
1663 Liberty Drive
Bloomington, IN 47403 USA
www.authorhouse.co.uk
UK TFN: 0800 0148641 (Toll Free inside the UK)
UK Local: 02036 956322 (+44 20 3695 6322 from outside the UK)

Because of the dynamic nature of the Internet, any web addresses or links contained in this book may have changed since publication and may no longer be valid. The views expressed in this work are solely those of the author and do not necessarily reflect the views of the publisher, and the publisher hereby disclaims any responsibility for them.

Any people depicted in stock imagery provided by Getty Images are models, and such images are being used for illustrative purposes only.
Certain stock imagery © Getty Images.

This book is printed on acid-free paper.

ISBN: 978-1-6655-8809-6 (sc)
ISBN: 978-1-6655-8808-9 (e)

Print information available on the last page.

Published by AuthorHouse 04/13/2023

Publishing Planned: 21/02/2021	1st. book	Completion: 05/05/2021
(Mother's Goodbye-World Anniversary ... '72)	Kublai Khan	(Kublai Coronation ... 05/05/1260)
(1st. Revise ... 08/12/2021)		(A Date Dear ... as 'twas a Day Dear)

Publishing Planned: 05/05/2021	2nd. book	Completion: 14/08/2021
(Kublai Khan's Coronation ... 05/05/1260)	'tween 9 'n 15	(Pak Independence ... 14/08/1947)
(1st Revision ... 29/10/2021)		(Myne Birth-Date ... 29/10/1941)

History of **Urdu** ... The **Mongol**/Turkish word **Urdu** means "**Camp**" or "**Palace**" ... Kublai ...

... **The Final Place of Rest** ... And That's How My Poëm Ends: Sadly ...

Awaiting; that the Loose End Breath, be shed,
'N downed he slept: Camp Urdu in bed,
That Spirits to the Ninth Heaven Arise.

(2008)

𝒯ariq   ℋameed

Introduction ... by Tariq Hameed ... Technical Analysis

In the **Purest** of Romantic Idioms, a Prophetic phrase stuns the Imagination! Revealing an Idea, a Plan ... such a Dream that Coleridge himself never managed to re-Capt. **Dream remained** Dream ...   True Till Today?
Pure Romanticism: **but** a Single Prophetic Word "War"? Ancestral voices prophesying war! Oh So Surprising???

Stage's Set ... let's Play? Captured by a total Un-Known? Declamation, Domination, Deterioration, Decline, Death!

TOTAL Respect for Coleridge Text, has been practiced ... till even the Line-End Punctuation ... including:

1. The 54 Original verses have been Repeated into 5 more Episodes ... 5 Periods of Kublai Khan's Life
2. These Independent Epochs, Respect Coleridge Rhyme, Rythm & Intonations ... slight Letter Changes
3. However, regarding the 54 Verses ... Pages:34/51: a Total Summary denotes ... 54 Individual Poëms
4. Likewise, regarding the 5 Periods ... Pages:59/63: in Full Historical Evidence ... 5 Individual Phases
5. To Validate the **Authenticity of Events**, all Periods References ... do Consult ... Pages:52/58 & 64/66

Homages ... by Myself ... **to my** Masters ... **who Built me** Future,

1. **My Mother** ... 'Mongst 1st. **Lady Doctors** (India) ... Gave me 100 Words to Memorise by Day ... **NO Errors!**
     Thus aged 9, I Knew the English Dictionary by Heart ♥! **A Voracious Reader** ... I Noted Every Word read!
2. **My Father** ... Titled "**Khan Sahib**" by *Exiting British*, for Services Rendered to *Election Laws* ... He Wrote,
     in 1952, "**Election Law**" for Pakistan ... which is still a **Reference Book**, in the **Supreme Court!**
3. **My Uncle** ... Scribe 'n **Hafiz-e-Qura'an** ... till Aged 20, Instructed me "**Atomic Letters**", in Urdu 'n English;
     Letter, Dot, Accent Separated: that 60 years later, I Created the "**Atomic** Wrist **Key-Board**"!
4. **My Servitor** ... **Ashraf** the Cross-Eyed; who Saw **Nothing, but** Knew Everything: Known 'n UnKnown!
     Excellent Story-Teller ... His Legend of "**Ogre Khumra and the** Rosy Færy", NEVER ended all 20 years!
5. **My Musician** ... Feroz Nizami ... Sweet, Soft 'n **Classical** ... Created the best Pak Film Tunes, in 50-tys
6. **My Theatre Writer** ... Syed Imtiaz Ali Taj ... Historical Personality ... *Died in my Arms*: God **Bless U!**
7. **My Loved Poët** ... Faiz Ahmed Faiz ... Poetry Lenin Prize, 1962! **Spoke** but little: **Smoked** but much!
8. **My Best Friend** ... Tanvir Ahmed Khan ... Born a day after, 78 years perfect ... in Respect Respected!
9. **My Calligrapher Adored** ... Ahmed Mirza Jamil ... "Think NOT with Brain; Think Wrist **not** Mind: Tariq"!

Tariq *Hameed*

(2000)

Voracious **R**eader 'n Searcher, since Two 'n Half years Old, of Where LYES the <u>TRUTH</u>? طارق حميد

"Aye, there Lyes the rub": so in this Hamlet of No Return, called 'World of the Wise Men of Gotham', only but be Bed-Ridden by the **Un-Wise of Bottom**, my small Wisdom but Swore faintly; "**Never** Truly **Grow-up**"!

'Twas **D**estiny, that born **Myopic**, Forced me to Imagine. Thus, <u>Truth</u> 'n **Purity** came to **Grasp**: it a day **dawned** that, "**D**irt were you Born, to returnest to Dirt": **Empty-Handed Come, Empty-Handed Gone** … so a lil by lil, formed a Philosophy: "**You only GAIN, what you GIVE**" …   Help **Humanity**; Not your own Self-Self!

Learning thus so early, that **Seeing was Un-**<u>Truth</u> … Lampions big of Light, Blinking 'n Flickering, so Blown-up in Multi-Fluid Colours in the Deep Depths of the Cosmos' … factually were, **Else-Things in the Else-Where?** Where? Questions to be Posed 'n **A**nswered: allowing the use of other Senses, like Sounds, Taste, Smell 'n Movements, in Truth to just Re-Construct the feasible **Probable Reality**; Intuitively analysing the Crayoned cricks 'n cracks of chalky traits, I justly Heard, the *Black-Board Talk back to me*: 'n Revealed by Mag♪c, the **Writing on the Wall** …
                    so Un-Veiled, the False-h**oo**d of the **Persons of Convenience**?

567 Words … **A Single Phrase** … **No** Punctuation Mark

41.   (<u>Vaticano</u>)   S W A L L O W S   *no punctuation*   Visions-3- 1993 Org. thBk-E-5b p-044--168-

a swarm   of
              swallows behind a **swarm** of *swallows* and
      when you turned the **other**   **way** round another **swarm**
            of *swallows* **rapidly**   **changing** itself into a different **swarm**
                  of *swallows* **which** rose up in the sky like smoke with veils in *front*
                        and veils in the back when they turn and squirm and float *like*
                              one body and a unique serpentine body going up and ***down***
                        and side to side then turning and returning becoming thicker ***and***
                  thinner and even more thinner than thin and suddenly transforming
      back to thicker and thicker when they turn to return to the point where
      they started to end not but to continue their play their game playing in
hordes of happiness of individual but united units of thousands of
differences so exceptionally knit together in harmony that only words
    and mere words lacked to describe them as you see them and hear them
        and feel them in their multiple beauty but such a multiple beauty that
            could be pointed out in every individual *swallow* which followed ***its***
                  own individual path and its own individual destiny but at the ***same***

... New **Writ** Technique Perusal **Scan/Read** ... VIBG OR ... RA NBOW ... **Words** in a **Page** only : in a ½ **Minute** ...

Noor-us-samaawat.com   **Qr-Thoughts**   **Site of** Tariq Hameed   www.noor-us-samaawat.com

Bcok 0   Volume 0

Volume 0 ...   (Poëm ... Kublai ... Khan) ...

...   2017   2021   ...

Revolutionary Grammar MIRACLE ... 270 Lines Re-Used ... in 54 Poetic Episod

English is myne Mystress   ...   Tariq   Hameed

(**Beowulf**) ... An Anglo-Saxon EPIC Poëm ...

Colour Code ... on Page -132--159-

Dedicated to :

... **I R I S** ... **Blue-Eyed** Blond ... **Who I N**ever **Found** ...

... **Perfect** **W**oman ... **Who Me N**ever **Found** ...

or perhaps

to **K**now to **L**earn to Live ?   do then **Try,,** to **Read** my **Bcoks** !!!

Without any **Harm,,** nor to **Self,** or to **NoOne** !!!   **Sans** faire **Mal** ni à **Soi,,** ni à **Personne** !

Please Study Pages -63/64--115- for 'pause' (,,) ... *'tween 9 'n 15*   *thBk-E-01*9-15*.pdf

KUBLA KHAN: TEXT OF THE POËM

Kubla Khan by **Samuel Taylor Coleridge**	*Or a Vision in a Dream. A Fragment*

Samuel Taylor Coleridge

Born on October 21, 1772 / Died on July 25, 1834

https://www.pexels.com/Samuel+Taylor+Coleridge

- Contents
- Biography
- Poems /208/
- Quotes /117/
- Comments /0/
- Project Gutenberg

Samuel Taylor Coleridge: born in Ottery St. Mary on 21 October 1772, youngest of ten children of John Coleridge (minister) and Ann Bowden Coleridge. Often bullied, mother remaining distant, Samuel quit house at 7. Found so by a neighbour, later the events of this horror night, showed frequently in his poëms and night visions, most of his adult life. His father died in 1781, and Samuel was sent to a **London** charity school for the clergy's children.

Coleridge was of ill health in summer 1797; so retired to a lonely farm house 'tween Porlock & Linton, on Exmoor confines (Somerset & Devonshire). A slight indisposition, the anodyne prescribed, of druggist effect, made him fall asleep; while reading the following sentence, in Purchas's Pilgrimage: "**Here the Khan Kubla commanded a palace to be built, and a stately garden thereunto: and thus ten miles of fertile ground were enclosed with a wall.**" In these 3 hours of profound sleep, with vivid confidence, he composed 'tween 200 to 300 lines: where **images rose up as objects**, producing parallel conscious-less expressions. On awaking: taking pen, ink, & paper, wrote the verses here preserved. **Unfortunately, awoken by the bell**; to his mortification, **the Dream & Vision, had Crumpled to Dust**!

Just as Left Fluid Images, but alas: without any after Restoration of the Real:

> ....Then all the charm
> Is broken -- all that phantom-world so fair,
> Vanishes, and a thousand circlets spread,
> And each mis-shape the other. Stay awhile,
> Poor youth! who scarcely dar'st lift up thine eyes--
> The stream will soon renew its smoothness, soon
> The visions will return! And lo! he stays.
> And soon the fragments dim of lovely forms
> Come trembling back, unite, and now once more
> The pool becomes a mirror.

Yet from the still surviving recollections of his mind, the Author has frequently purposed to finish for himself what had been originally, as it were, given to him … but the to-morrow is yet to come …

<u>Nota</u>: **Now Completed 225 years later, by T.H.** …

(As a contrast to this vision, I have annexed a fragment of a very different character, describing with equal fidelity the dream of pain and disease.--1816.)

© by owner. Provided: at no charge for educational purposes. & **this tomorrow has now become … T.H. Tnkx.**

MY PHILOSOPHY	MA PHILOSOPHIE
IN LIFE	EN VIE
...	...
EVERYONE'S GUILTY	TOUS COUPABLES
UNLESS	SI NON
PROVED INNOCENT	PROUVÉ INNOCENT
...	...
THUS	AINSI
I HAVE	JE N'AI
NEVER	JAMAIS
SUFFERED	SOUFFERT
IN THIS WORLD	EN CE MONDE

... What They Taught Me: 'n How ...

My Father ... Election Commissioner: received many Political Parties Presents; all Pervaded without Pity! 'Twas strictly forbidden, to All 'n One, to touch anything in-coming! Once I took an Orange 'n Paid a 3 days Preclusion: Only Oranges! Thus, Learnt I ... the 11th. Commandment ... THOU shalt NOT CHEAT thy EAT!

My Mother ... 1st. Lady Doctors, of the Continent: one day, she murmured in the kitchen, with a school-mate; so asked, what 'twas? "You owe him 3 cents"! "I owe No-Thing to No-One? Pay, 'n I jump 10 meters"! Him sent off, she asked, "Why Risk your Life, Son"? "Or I Respect what you Teach me? Or am Lyer? Both Ways, such Life's NOT worth Living! Thus, Learnt I ... the 12th. Commandment ... THOU shalt NOT SELL thy Soul!

My Writs belong to the beYond ... Gifts must be Gifted ... U r Allowed Free Use ? On Condition ? Plz, Quote Te !

Born: **29**th. October, 1941 ...   **Tariq**   Naturalised French   ...   **16/01/19**78

Papa: Khan Sahib Mian Abdul   **Hameed**   Hijrat Authorised : <u>**Pakistan**</u>   ...   **16/01/20**11

Mama: Bégum Méraj Hameed   **Suharwardi**   UK Accorded : Join Family   ...   **15/01/20**15

Sis: **Tahira** Hameed   ... 01/03/1943

Bros: Mian **Kausar** Hameed   ... **16/01/19**48   ...   **Papa pass**   ...   16/01/19<u>57</u>

Server: **Ashraf** Mian Bihari   ... Teller & Confident (**Illiterate**)   ... "Bury **me in** Thorns **as in** Life"

Ustad   My Masters

1.   **Hafiz M**uhammad **A**zeem   (**T**aught **S**cript,**T**hink,**Hon**our)   ...   **Scribe of** Qura'an **(Uncle)**

2.   Feroz **Nizami**   (always offered me a cup of tea)   ...   **¶**us♪c **(Classic)**

3.   **F**aiz Ahmed **F**aiz   (a chain smoker)   ...   Poetry (Lenin Prize, 1962)

4.   **S**yed **I**mtiaz Ali **T**aj   (**D**ied in my **a**rms)   ...   Theater (Writer **&** History of)

5.   **A**hmed Mirza **J**amil   (**T**hink **W**rist not **M**ind)   ...   Noori Nastaliq (Calligraphy)

          (He invented the Modern 'Fonts' in **Urdu** *& Arab)*

{T **'Atomic'**:   based on studies of **Hazarat** Ameer **Khusro** ... Darbar-e Balban, 1272}

Primary: St. Anthony's High School ... **Lahore**

University: Government College (Ravians) ... **Lahore**, **Punjab**

Advanced: Institute of 'Chartered Accountants' ... **England** & **Wales**

International: Systems of Production (on Computer: '69-'74) ... **Europe**: Latin (South)

Global Primary   <u>**National.Chart.of.Accounts.fr**</u> **on Computer** {*}

1.   M.I.S. (Industrial Giant : **BSN**) {*}   1970   ... Fabrication (Glass) : *Paris*. {*}

2.   M.I.S. Data-Bases : Liquids (Ciba-Geigy)   1973   ... *Basel*, *Schweiz* (Chemistry)

Inventions

3.   '**Atomic**' **Urdu** & Arab Alphabet   ...   <u>**Unicode**.org Consortium</u>

4.   '**Atomic**' **Urdu** Key-Board (Computer)   ...   <u>NADRA Nat. IDs +200 Millions</u>

5.   '**Atomic**' **Urdu** Computer (Localisation)   ...   <u>**Microsoft** : Atomic Alphabet</u>

Concepts   ...   **Q**uod **E**rat **D**emonstrandum ... *Euclid*

6.   **Qura'an** Evolutive **D**imensionnal **s**tructure   ...   **QED**s **Vahis** Revealed ...

7.   **Qura'an** Translation **M**ethodologies **s**implified   ...   **QTM**s **W**ord under **W**ord ...

(The Third & <u>**Multi-Dimensions**</u> ... of the Qura'ani Structure "Revealed")

| ♫♪ ut .♫uhu♫♪ | email : <br> harf.noor@gmail.com | email : thuqky@yahoo.com <br> email : thuqky@gmail.com | N^{oo}R^{us} Sam^{aa}waT |

Né : **29ème.** Octobre, 1941 ... **Tariq** Naturalisé Français ... **16/01/1978**

Père : Khan Sahib Mian Abdul Hameed Hijrat Autorisé : **Pakistan** ... **16/01/2011**

Mère : Bégum Méraj Hameed **Suharwardi** GB Accord : Joindre Famille ... **15/01/2015**

Sœur : **Tahira** Hameed ... 01/03/1943

Frère : Mian Kausar Hameed ... **16/01/1948** ... **Père** part ... 16/01/1957

Serviteur : **Ashraf** Mian Bihari ... Raconteur & Fidèle (**Illettré**) ... "**Comme la** Vie, Enterre-**moi en** Épines"

Ustad Mes Maîtres

1. **H**afiz **M**uhammad **A**zeem (Maître Script,Pensée,Hon ur) ... **Scribe de Qura'an (Oncle)**

2. Feroz **Nizami** (m'offrait toujours une tasse de thé) ... **M**us**i**que **(Classique)**

3. **Faiz** Ahmed **Faiz** (fumer en chaine) ... Poésie (Prix Lénine, 1962)

4. **S**yed **I**mtiaz Ali **T**aj (Mort dans mes **b**ras) ... Théâtre (Écrivain, Histoire d')

5. **Ahmed** Mirza **Jamil** (Penser Poignée pas Bête) ... Noori Nastaliq (Calligraphie)

*(Il a invent*é des 'Polices' Modernes en **Urdu** & Arabe*)*

{TH '**Atomic**' : basé sur les œuvres de **Hazarat** Ameer Khusro ... Darbar de Balban, 1272}

Premier : St. Anthony's High School ... **Lahore**

Université : Government College (Ravians) ... **Lahore**, **Punjab**

Supérieur : Institute of ' Chartered Accountants ' ... **England** & **Wales**

Internationale : Systèmes de Production (sur Ordinateur '69-'74) ... **Europe** : Latine (Sud)

Premier Globale **<u>National.Chart.of.Accounts.fr</u> sur Ordinateur** {*}

1. M.I.S. (Géant Industriel : **BSN**) {*} 1970 ... Fabrication (Verres) : *Paris.* {*}

2. M.I.S. Base de Données : Liquides (Ciba-Geigy) 1973 ... *Basel*, *Schweiz* (Chimie)

Inventions

3. '**Atomique**' **Urdu** & Arab Alphabet ... **<u>Unicode</u>**.org Consortium

4. '*Atomique*' **Urdu** Clavier (Ordinateur) ... <u>NADRA Nat. IDs +200 Millions</u>

5. '**Atomique**' **Urdu** Ordinateur (Localisation) ... **Microsoft :** Alphabet Atomique

Concepts ... Quod Erat Demonstrandum ... *Euclid*

6. **Qu**r**a'an** Evolutive **D**imensionnelle **s**tructure ... **QED**s Vahis Révélés ...

7. **Qu**r**a'an** Traduction **M**éthodologies **s**implifiées ... **QTM**s **Mot** sous **Mot** ...

(Troisième & **<u>Multi-Dimensions</u>** ... de la Structure **Q**ura'anique "Revélé")

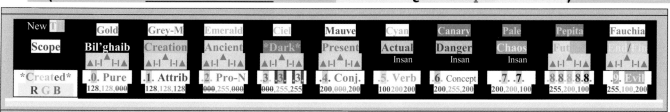

The Original Kublai Khan ... of S.T. Coleridge

Kublai Khan (occasionally spelled Kubla Khan) and his empire prompted wild flights of fancy among Europeans from the time of Marco Polo's expedition of 1271-1292. But who was the Great Khan, really? A romantic vision of Kublai Khan's realm came to English poet Samuel Taylor Coleridge in an opium-laced dream, inspired by reading the account of a British traveller and describing the city as Xanadu.

S.T. Coleridge, *Kubla Khan*, 1797

....Stanza 1

1.

In Xanadu did Kubla Khan
A stately pleasure-dome decree:
Where **Alph**, the sacred river, ran
Through caverns measureless to man
Down to a sunless sea.

6.
So twice five miles of fertile ground
With walls and towers were girdled round:
And there were gardens bright with sinuous rills,
Where blossomed many an incense-bearing tree;
And here were forests ancient as the hills,
Enfolding sunny spots of greenery.

....Stanza 2

12.
But oh! that deep romantic chasm which slanted
Down the green hill athwart a cedarn cover!
A savage place! as holy and enchanted
As e'er beneath a waning moon was haunted
By woman wailing for her demon-lover!

17.
And from this chasm, with ceaseless turmoil seething,
As if this earth in fast thick pants were breathing,
A mighty fountain momently was forced:
Amid whose swift half-intermitted burst
Huge fragments vaulted like rebounding hail,
Or chaffy grain beneath the thresher's flail:
And 'mid these dancing rocks at once and ever
It flung up momently the sacred river.

25.
Five miles meandering with a mazy motion
Through wood and dale the sacred river ran,
Then reached the caverns measureless to man,
And sank in tumult to a lifeless ocean:
And 'mid this tumult Kubla heard from far
Ancestral voices prophesying war!

31.
The shadow of the dome of pleasure
Floated midway on the waves;
Where was heard the mingled measure
From the fountain and the caves.
It was a miracle of rare device,
A sunny pleasure-dome with caves of ice!

....Stanza 3

37.
A damsel with a dulcimer
In a vision once I saw;
It was an Abyssinian maid,
And on her dulcimer she played,
Singing of **Mount Abora**.

42.
Could I revive within me
Her symphony and song,
To such a deep delight 'twould win me,
That with music loud and long,
I would build that dome in air,
That sunny dome! those caves of ice!

48.
And all who heard should see them there,
And all should cry, Beware! Beware!
His flashing eyes, his floating hair!
Weave a circle round him thrice,
And close your eyes with holy dread,
For he on honey-dew hath fed,
And drunk the milk of Paradise.
54.

.......................Then all the charm
Is broken -- all that phantom-world so fair,
Vanishes, and a thousand circlets spread,
And each mis-shape the other. Stay awhile,
Poor youth! who scarcely dar'st lift up thine eyes--
The stream will soon renew its smoothness, soon
The visions will return! And lo! he stays,
And soon the fragments dim of lovely forms
Come trembling back, unite, and now once more
     The Pool becomes a Mirror.

Per vedere l'Originale (For the Original of) Kublai Khan ... -10--115- & -11--115-

Kublai Khan (talvolta scritto Kubla Khan) e il suo impero provocarono folli voli di fantasia tra gli Europei dal tempo della spedizione di Marco Polo del 1271-1292. Ma chi era il Gran Khan, davvero? Una visione romantica del regno di Kublai Khan giunse al poeta inglese Samuel Taylor Coleridge in un sogno intriso di oppio, ispirato dalla lettura del racconto di un viaggiatore britannico e descrivendo la città come Xanadu. S.T. Coleridge, *Kubla Khan*, 1797

....Stanza 1

1.

In Xanadu il Kubla Khan

Un magnifico plazzo con duomo decreta:
Dove **Alph**, fiume d'aqua sacra, in mezzo del camin
Dove i uomoni passano i caverni sensa dimension
Andando a un mare sensa sole laciando ogni speranza.

6.

Due volte cinque miglia di terra fertile ronde
I muri e torri cinti in rotond:
E c'erano giardini luminosi di sinuosi ruscelli,
Dove sbocciarono l'incenso dei alberi tanti;
E dove fiorirono le foreste e colline antiche,
Avvolgendo le macchie di soleggiante verde.

....Stanza 2

12.

Ma oh! quale profondo baratro romantico obliquo
Traversando la verde collina sotto copertura di cedro!
Un luogo selvaggio di fate! santo e incantato
Sempre sotto come una luna ossessionata calante
Come una donna piangendo per il suo demone-amante!

17.

E da questo baratro, con incessante tumulto ribollente,
Come se la terra in sorsi veloci e densi era respirante,
Una potente fontana fu brevemente forzata:
Mezzo al cui il rapido scoppio era interrotto a metà
Volteggiavano grandine rimbalzante enormi frammenti,
E sotto il flagello-trebbiatrice di pula, cadeva i granelli:
Che in mezzo a queste rocce danzanti allo stesso tempo
Dunque alzò in un attimo le onde del fiume sacro.

25.

Cinque miglia serpeggianti con un movimento intricato
Attraverso boschi e valli scorreva il fiume sacro,
Poi raggiunse le caverne incommensurabili per l'uomo,
E affondò in tumulto in un oceano senza vita:
E' in mezzo-tumulto che ha sentito da lontano Kubla
                    Voci ancestrali profetizzano la guera!

31.

Nel ombra della cupola dei piaceri
Galleggiava a metà tra le onde;
Dove si udì la mista misura
Dalla fontana alle grotte.
È stato un miracolo di dispositivo raro,
Puro piacere, cupola soleggiata con grotte di ghiaccio!

....Stanza 3

37.

Una damigela con un dulcimer
Una visione una sola volta che ho visto;
Era una abissina signiorina,
E sul suo dulcimer ha suonato,
Il Canto del Monte Abora.

42.

Potrei ristabilire dentro di me
La sua sinfonia del suo canto,
Un piacere così profondo mi avrà conquistato,
Che come musica forte e lunga,
Costruirei quella cupola ariosa nell'aria,
Quella cupola solare! quelle grotte di ghiaccio!

48.

E tutti che hanno sentito dovrebbero vederli li,
E che tutti piangenno, Attenzione! Attenzione!
I suoi occhi lampeggianti, e i capelli fluttuanti!
A lui intrecci un cerchio intorno volte tre,
Poi chiudi gli occhi con santo terrore,
Poiché di rugiada di miele si è nutrito,
E bevuto il latte del Paradiso.

54.

........................Poi tutto il fascino
Si è rotto -- tutto quel mondo fantasma così bello,
Svanisce, e mille cerchietti si diffondono,
E ognuno deforma l'altro. Rimanere un po,
Povero giovane! che appena osi alzare un occhio--
Il torrente presto rinnoverà la sua dolcezza, presto
Le visioni torneranno! Ed ecco! lui resta, pronto
E presto i frammenti di belle forme si oftuscano
Unisciti, e ora ancora una volta, torna tremante indietro
    Le Piscina diventa uno Specchio.

https://www.pexels.com/search/Beijing/ …

https://www.pexels.com/photo/multicolored-concrete-building-with-a-lake-view-showing-the-distinct-architectural-design-of-ancient-china-2846005/

https://www.pexels.com/search/Beijing/

https://www.pexels.com/photo/people-riding-on-boat-2845970/

That.Spirits.to.the.Ninth.Heaven.Arise…   Beethoven's.9th.Sympohony.first.recording.(Bruno.Seidler-Winkler,1923)

Beethoven's.9th.Sympohony.(Hymn.to.Joy)…https://www.youtube.com/watch?v=nZV2EuA9fwM

================================='n thus carries on … Tariq Hameed=================================

https://unsplash.com/

photo-1483135349295-9e3c48106ee6.jpg

(Spring Mountain)

English Rendering … by … Tariq Hameed

On Fragrant Hill in a cosy season of Spring, I ascended
To meet the Golden Face; on a Peak I climbed and Mounted
Where Flowers bright in rainy RAINBOW's shone 'n gleamed 'n Smiled
Scenting incensed Smoke, as blessed LIGHT; hazy mists wafted!

Bamboos of jade, bubbles rain-dropping, fell fast on big Rock's edge
Winds blowing piping songs 'mongst green Pines on passing Mount's wedge:
Thus 'fore Buddha's Temple Devine, conducted I the incense ceremony on ledge;
So back on way, I rode the Blue-Dragon, in the Royal carriage's bridge

Vision of Kublai Khan … in Octet form.

Longevity Hill in Beijing, where Kublai Khan wrote his poëm

https://pixabay.com/photos/dragon-3d-fantasy-legend-fairytale-5163218/ … Free Photo … **Dragon**

https://images.unsplash.com/photo-1483135349295-9e3c48106ee6?ixid=MXwxMjA3fDB8MHxwaG90by1wYWdlfHx8fGVufDB8fHw%3D&ixlib=rb-1.2.1&auto=format&fit=crop&w=800&q=80 … Free Photo … Xanadu   … Free Photo … Dragon

時膺韶景陟蘭峰
不憚躋攀謁粹容
花色映霞祥彩混
壚煙拂霧瑞光重

雨霑瓊干巖邊竹
風襲琴聲嶺際松
淨刹玉毫瞻禮罷
回程仙駕馭蒼龍

Kublai Khan, was well educated in diverse languages; also simultaneously had a good mastery of the Chinese poetry. Unfortunately, most of his works survived not. However, one of his Chinese poëm, was included in an old Selection of Yuan Poetry (元詩選). It was titled by Kublai himself … as 'Inspiration recorded while enjoying an ascent to the Holy Spring Mountain'. This poëm through multiple translations: starting Mongolian, then into Cyrillic and others; finally was handed down to us. Historians say, "**Once in Spring, Kublai Khan decided to worship in a famous Buddhist Temple, in a Summer Resort in Western Khanbaliq**". (Beijing Region)!

On his way back, ascending the renowned **Longevity Hill** (Mongolian name Tumen Nast Uul); 'twas divinely inspired, to write this poëm ... That's what Coleridge was reading; when falling asleep ... Dream Unfinished! Finished by TH!

… Tariq Hameed … Completion & End … Kublai Khan …

==============================='n thus carries on … Tariq Hameed===============================

....Stanza 1

1.

In 'tis Shangtu did Kublai Khan

Where berged Maiden Maids with Harps in glee:

Softly lo, did Saintly Spirits scan

Thru twisted teases, Endless Gifts to van

Away onto a Timeless spree.

6.

Ran miles 'n miles of goodly downed

Where ups 'n downs of Fortunes un-mound:

Where Flowers Sprouted, Light 'n oft, in Laughs still,

Spring spurted in Myriad a Sense, happy to be;

Troubled Jungles of Past, 'twere Old to us as until,

Englobing Sun 'n moon: in multi-lands færie.

....Stanza 2

12.

Dream Charms so, Sombre faded; depth instated

O'er Spaced scenes in Falls 'n Rocks, sad browns hover!

Magsc Spells enlarged, Pure as 'twas dis-Chanted

Mystery bathed Mounting moon, e'er be shunted

So vile Witches unveil their Demonic cover!

17.

Unto an Abyss, with breezeless Voids a-whirling,

As Life, 'tis last ticks 'n throbs was weaning,

Lofty in disdain, momentarily was grossed:

=='n thus carries on … Tariq Hameed===

Sharp 'n Mortal, fell a fully-pungent thrust
Firm fractions flew, so reSounding Ô a Wail,
Of fluffy Pain; held on Closed pinged Lips so Frail:
Stuck 'mid these frenzied flocks, for now or never
Struggling but momentarily; down the flowing River.

25.

Wonder wanders, Nature 'n Souls; of prime traction
In woods, Vales 'n Dells; did 'tis dusked Waters span,
Lost 'tween breached Taverns, hues meaningful to Man,
'Tis Muse sunk in spoils, Ô so de Void a motion:
This hubbub during … Kublai, hear did afar
                              Ancestral voices prophesying war!

31.

Rising off the Hades of the Shades of measure
Bloating half-way unto the Caves;
Interred 'twas a Tingled Treasure
Dug in high Mounts, 'n inlaid Graves.
Mirages in sleep, of darkened revise,
Fate's dubious Leisure-doom, Destined to slice!

....Stanza 3

37.

Floating Sad Airs, so Soft 'n fair
Hallucination blurred, I be-saw;C
'Twas 'twas of an Oriental trade,

=='n thus carries on … Tariq Hameed===

Dreamet ♪otes, that **no** Treason betrayed,
Chanting of **Count Alora**.

42.
Relief so strung unto me
Writ in ♪otes Stringed in a Throng,
Sunk in Profound Thoughts t♦♦, to rim me,
Aye Pain in Melody, 'n in **Song**,
Bound to a Throne full of flair,
Where **Enemies** Sing 'n **Friends** Malice!

48.
But who heard not, sat wither thither near,
Hearers Cries Crying Called! Aware! Beware!
Eyes all did smash, in gloat 'n in blare!
In Mag♪c circles, wove once twice thrice,
Firm Blank Open eyes, unHoly Dead,
L♦♦se honeyed dews, which **never** spread,
Hark, Ô milks 'n brews which Ecstasise.
54.

Evolution: Great Wars of the Great Kublai … The Youthful … Early Period … Afore Ilkhanate

---

Ilkhan means **Viceroy**, title of *Hulagu* son of Tolui, *grandson* of Genghis, younger *brother* of Möngké: third brother being **Kublai**, the so Great Mongol Khan (1260-1294), who later controlled the post **Song** North China. Hulagu … ordered to administer full Mongol rule over then **West Asia**, from 1253 CE, mobilised to expand to Iran and Iraq; crushed the ruling Ismailites (named "**Assassins**", originally "**Hashish** Sellers". Abbasid Caliph (**adoring Diamonds**), collapsed by Hulagu: rapid capture of Baghdad. Executing the Caliph (**eat Gems**), a week-long slaughter Killed 800,000, as per tradition; immense a Syrian

==='n thus carries on … Tariq Hameed==

Massacre followed: "**Halaku**" now synonym of "Killer" … is common coin in **Urdu**!

This Name lingers on in "Urdu": Pakistan and India … instituted in Mongol/Mughal Rule (**1526 to 1857**).

By end decade, Mongols self-divided into three distinct Khanates, ruled by the many branches of Genghis' successors: named generally, the **Ilkhantes** …

Chagatai Khanate, <u>Golden.Horde</u>; and **Yuan Dynasty** of Great Kublai Khan!

Kublai as young, Lived in a **Round Tent**, named "**Yurt**" (Round … **Genghis**' was **Square**: Urdu). Really, Who were the **Mongols**? Originated by Unification of Nomadic Clans: from many diverse regions of the then Central Mongolia. When Kublai was born, Genghis' Empire, extended, from a **Sea Caspian** to an **Ocean Pacific**: conquering Yen-Ching (Beijing)! Thus, when his uncle Ögödei became the Great Khan, he trusted Kublai a fiefdom of about 10,000 households, which he administered by proxy …

but soon directly … realising the injustice Imposed by the Imposed Rulers!

Ögödei: third son of Genghis Khan and Borte Ujin … Genghis Khan knew that Ögödei had a courteous and generous character. His charisma explains his success to keep the Empire on his father Genghis' path. Ögödei was a pragmatist, and the affairs of Mongol Empire remained largely stable during his reign. He had no delusions that he was Genghis' equal as Military Commander/Organizer; but he had the knack to well use abilities of those he found mostly capable.

......................Then all the charm Is broken -- all that phantom-world so fair, Vanishes, and a thousand circlets spread, And each mis-shape the other. Stay awhile, Poor youth! who scarcely dar'st lift up thine eyes- The stream will soon renew its smoothness, soon The visions will return! And lo! he stays, And soon the fragments dim of lovely forms Come trembling back, unite, and now once more The **Pool becomes a Mirror**.	......................Then all the charm is broken -- all that phantom-world so fair, Vanishes, and a thousand circlets spread, And each mis-shape the other. Stay awhile, Poor youth! who scarcely dar'st lift up thine eyes- The stream will renew its smoothness soon, soon The visions will return! And lo! he stays, And soon the fragments dim of lovely forms Come trembling back, unite, and now once more That **Pool becomes a Mirror** and boon.

Yet from the still surviving recollections of his mind, the Author has frequently purposed to finish for himself what had been originally, as it were, given to him … but the to-morrow is yet to come …

Episode 1 … Nota: **Now Completed 225 years later, by T.H.** …

(As a contrast to this vision, I have annexed a fragment of a very different character, describing with equal fidelity the dream of pain and disease.--1816.)

& **this tomorrow has now become**

… T.H. Tnkx.

....Stanza 1

1.

In Xanadu did Kubla Khan

Ô Lo beheld Towers aroused to Skies yond Sea:
Limpid Pools become Mirrors full plan
Thru torrid whirl-p**o**ols, of Wars cleft as can
As Boundless as Bounds could be.

6.

Stirred once mazes 'n dazes of Horrid Sound
Lost Losses 'n wins, when Battles abound:
Destruct Smiles Never; or Never more'll lift or till,
But Gonged Wars a-Destined; Die or Live 'n be;
Sad a story, Tender of Old; to Dream as will,
At Start, lots of Glory: to flatter Warlords eerie.

....Stanza 2

12.

Destructs Drastic, oh Sorts; in Dry Ruins Pained
Up-Hill 'n Down-Vale, whispers 'n Revolts rover!
Pit King 'gainst King ... brothers in arms dis-mantled
Err's Human, in Being 'n Battle; Hope undaunted
While, Ô wily Women; Wailed their vain endeavour!

17.

Lo Cry; no Rhyme nor theme! Revolts Void unmeaning,
In throes 'n flicks so sinks the World ... Reeling,
L**o**osers not Ch**o**osers, in deep Thought engrossed:

Book ... *thBk-E-01*9-15*.pdf-019- طارق حميد THINKS 'n THOUGHTS -019--115-

... Tariq Hameed ... Completion & End ... Kublai Khan ...
=============================='n thus carries on ... Tariq Hameed==============================

Win or lose, or lose to win! **Ends** the last burst
Arms, swords 'n arrows; came but to **Null** avail,
Bound to be; bent to bend: no flee no ship no sail:
Prisoned in shocks 'n mocks forever, in **never** in ever ever
Flung deep in dungy-holes; Heart 'n Soul in sever.

25.

Bent Kublai to win; too win, in swift reaction
In Arts 'n Craft, 'n in base 'n higher plan,
Set unto poor 'n rich, 'n just 'n fair; as can,
Putting in place, Thoughts 'n Thinks; in emptive action:
Drum-beats; that none but Kublai heard: far so far
Ancestral voices prophesying war!

31.

Hardened Shades of Strife; nor Peace nor leisure
To lye to sleep, all in their Graves;
To Dream perchance, in minced Pleasure
Dead interred be, Ô Ancient Slaves.
But Kublai was Wise; 'n no fool, nor novice,
Thus Chance in Life 'n Luck, threw he to Dice!

....Stanza 3

37.

Knowing how to trick Lucifer
That off 'n on beamed, all but raw;

====================================='n thus carries on ... Tariq Hameed=====================================

So Dawned Light of help 'n aid,
'N Engels' Harps, Sweetened Chants strayed,
Humming of Charmed Pandora.

42.

Dawn, high Dawn; revive within me
Triple Destiny! Sounding 'tis gong, gong, gong,
When 'tis done, 'tis done: can't undone be,
Be it a King or a Kong,
Thus Lion Lioness down laid; in theirs' lair,
'Twas a Lone-dome: in Fortune's 'twain Device!

48.

Apart those who heard, be they anywhere,
Here There, or in the After-Where!
Ô Courage aBound, be fair to be-fair!
Round go Mysteries, where Phantoms do slice,
Darkened fixed gaze, NO Thoughts in 'tis head,
Gone with the Wind; in Death's good Old Wed,
That, Paradise or Hell be any-Wise.
54.

Evolution: Great Wars of the Great Kublai … First WAR … Middle Period (Part 1) … The Ilkhanate

At Genghis' advice, Sorkhotani chose a Buddhist woman as Kublai's nurse. Genghis Khan also performed a ritual for his first hunt at nine years old, when he Killed a rabbit and an antelope; smearing per the Mongol customs, the animal's fat, on the mid finger: saying "All Ye! **Heed the words of this young boy**; so full of wisdom". Genghis died! Kublai's father Tolui served for a couple of years as regent … then his uncle, Ögödei was enthroned. When Mongols conquered the **Jins**, Ögödei gifted Kublai his own estate. However inexperienced, he reigned by proxy; corruption resulted by an ingrained and **self-help**, 'put in pocket' official's excessive taxation: huge Chinese peasants' flocks flight; resulting in Tax losses! Kublai wisely intervening rapidly, reformed with newer officials, helping the previously fled peasants, to return.

Kublai since the early years, was greatly amorous of Chinese Art and Culture; so invited a prominent Buddhist monk, Haiyun to his Mongol "**Urdu**" (Camp) ... Kublai's always Wise and Sage endeavours, to '**Balance the Opposites**', engaged diverse Nationalities ... respectfully: *Buddhist, Christens and Muslims*.

Ordered in 1253 attacking Yunnan, he requested submission. Ruling, Dali-Gao family murdered his team. The Mongol East Wing went to Sichuan Basin: West Wing to West Sichuan: and Kublai went over southern grasslands, to take the capital city of **Dali** (Old Tali: Yunnan): strangely & wisely, he spared the residents, his envoy's slayers. The Dali King defected, surrendering the use of his forces ... Wisely, Duan Xingzhi, last Dali King, was named local ruler (**Tusi**); a pacification officer also appointed ... Peace, Ô Peace, lasted not long? **Kublai departed and Trouble broke**! Unrest arose 'mongst certain factions. However, Xingzhi pacified the court; offering Möngké detail maps of Yunnan: and likewise counselled on the methodology of the vanquishing of the resisting tribes ... and he also furnishing the Mongol army, many guides, deploys and vanguards. Before end 1256, Uryankhadai's armies had pacified Yunnan.

......................Then all the charm Is broken -- all that phantom-world so fair, Vanishes, and a thousand circlets spread, And each mis-shape the other. Stay awhile, Poor youth! who scarcely dar'st lift up thine eyes- The stream will soon renew its smoothness, soon The visions will return! And lo! he stays, And soon the fragments dim of lovely forms Come trembling back, unite, and now once more The **Pool becomes a Mirror**.	......................Then all the charm is broken -- all that phantom-world so fair, Vanishes, and myriads of circlets spread, And each mis-shape the other. Stay awhile, Poor youth! who scarcely dar'st lift up thine eyes- The stream will renew its smoothness soon, soon The visions will return! And lo! he stays, And soon the fragments dim lost loving forms Come trembling back, unite, and now once more That **Pool becomes a Mirror** and boon.

Yet from the still surviving recollections of his mind, the Author has frequently purposed to finish for himself what had been originally, as it were, given to him ... but the to-morrow is yet to come ...

Episode 2 ... Nota: **Now Completed 225 years later, by T.H.** ...

(As a contrast to this vision, I have annexed a fragment of a very different character, describing with equal fidelity the dream of pain and disease.--1816.)

... T.H. Tnkx.

==='n thus carries on ... Tariq Hameed==

....Stanza 1

1.

In 'tis Shangtu did Kublai Khan

      A day Sensed War drums, in ears eyes Presence be:

      In Mage Images, of Strife, of Destruct 'n ban

      Brothers blew Brothers, Swords slew Swords as clan

      To Sink in a deep Senseless plea.

6.

      For days in a haze of Horror Bound

      Lost gains Sound, when hounds go round:

      Flowers petal only, where God's will's God's will,

      So left to Die, to Die; then good God's will 'twill be;

      In forlorn Forests destroyed, oft of War's torn mill,

      Thus Kings 'n Crowns fall down; tread 'n weary.

....Stanza 2

12.

Trust Failed: lo Falsed Struct! All Lost, 'n Null gained

      Ô Pain 'twas, well in vain; drawn Wars' rising Fever!

      Fist to fist, face to face; Ruined 'n dis-ventured

      Arc then Sword in hand, on foot on horse-back Mounted

Veiled wedded Widows, so watching their Sorts sour!

17.

      So came once a Dream! Conquer all of all leaning,

      By East by South; it be Strong, it be Weakling,

      Up then down, blew this Song? Unity de-crossed:

================================='n thus carries on ... Tariq Hameed================================

For win's but a win; ends as Dust, or it be Crust
Nor Fail nor flail; Noise dense: Ô Cry bewail,
Conquer 'n win! Be! Stopped Null a Wind, nor Gale:
Firm as a Rock; stiff as a Cliff: all in bevor
Surmounting but as Stars, in Firmament's Ether.

25.

A King winning a winning! Masterly action
Top Artful Craft; 'n in Wars of a lofty scan,
Rented Breaks; in Hates 'n stakes, of Man versus Man,
Tragic Acumen of Wisdom Wise; a Voiding all faction:
Pitter-a-pat; drummed Fate! Kublai eyed, away 'n far
                    Ancestral voices prophesying war!

31.

Shadows Shallow Strived: slitting lean a mean fissure
To be or be not ? Perish Ô Slaves;
Dingle to Dongle! Deep in pressure
Sombring so: Silent in Deadly Waves.
A Worldly wanderer; a-wondering thrice,
Risking, Life 'n Luck 'n Destined Chance, doubly twice!

. . . . Stanza 3

37.

In Life so short 'n Ephemere
Came this brief Dream, I that fore-saw;

To Softly Surely a bit did fade,

Heavenly Music, half notes inlaid,

Delving unto E.A.Poe's Eleonora.

42.

Aye Ô Sleep! Ope hidden Eye, to History

Just to See Ending, the Dynasty Song,

Turn full circle, Wheels; in Cries unHoly,

Bell Rings! Dreams un-tell! Ding 'n Dong,

Slept back unto Ma Nature's care,

Ô lo so, go to Hell ... lice, mice 'n Vice!

48.

Thunder Light or Rain, Bound 'n Bare,

So be discrete, try not to stare!

Vacant: in Pensive moods ... sharped Eclair!

Struck Lone, by Fortune's Magic Dice,

Never to awake: in bed or in spread,

Where bells tolled in a dark cold shed,

To Wisely our History to revise.

54.

Evolution: Great Wars of the Great Kublai ... Second WAR ... Middle Period (Part 2) ... Song Conquest

Kublai Khan: first Mongol to transform Mongol horsemen, as efficient and solid naval force, played a decisive role in the famous battle of Xiangyang (1267-73) ... turning-point in Mongol's long war against an established **Song** Dynasty's centuries old rule over China. All started in 1265, after Möngké's decade long but totally unsuccessful campaign against the **Songs**; where Kublai captured 146 **Song** warships in Sichuan battle. This early victory gave him the nucleus of his Mongol fleet. Kublai recognized quickly, that it was of vitally a great importance, mastering

=='n thus carries on ... Tariq Hameed===

Song's riverine superiority ... to quote a well-known ancient dictum, **"If 'twere existed no Yangtze River, 'twere be NO Songs existing!"** ...

> **adopting age-old traditions**, the Mongol armies were best known for their able horse-back agility ...
>> **but** Kublai's navy, furnished the formal blow: subjugating traditional China.

At outset, Kublai faced a dilemma insoluble, vividly expressed by a strong memorial by a Wisely Wise, old Chinese Sage, **"I have heard, one can conquer an empire on horseback, but can one govern it on horseback?"** China was **impossible, administered by Mongols inexperienced** ... Adoption of existing Chinese methods & patterns was obliged. That 'twas done to full extent, assuredly & slowly; retake established procedures: to extent of losing their personal identity. However, working through Chinese agents, they avoided to be alienated from the population masses; which could have rejected them at any moment ...

> (and that's what exactly happened later, in 1368).

The Mongols, numerically inferior, used to different patterns of life and less advanced culturally than Chinese, just **could not rule China for long, as a privileged distinct caste**. So, Kublai's historical personal decision was brilliant.

......................Then all the charm Is broken -- all that phantom-world so fair, Vanishes, and a thousand circlets spread, And each mis-shape the other. Stay awhile, Poor youth! who scarcely dar'st lift up thine eyes- The stream will soon renew its smoothness, soon The visions will return! And lo! he stays, And soon the fragments dim of lovely forms Come trembling back, unite, and now once more The **Pool becomes a Mirror**.	......................Then all the charm is broken -- all that random-world so rare, Vanishes, and myriads of circlets spread, For all shapes do mis-shape in time 'n while: Fool youth! who scarcely dar'st lift up thine eyes- The stream will renew its smoothness soon, soon The visions will return! And lo! he stays, And soon the fragments dim lost loving forms Come skipping back, untied, 'n vast more more That **Pool becomes a Mirror** and flan and boon.

Yet from the still surviving recollections of his mind, the Author has frequently purposed to finish for himself what had been originally, as it were, given to him ... but the to-morrow is yet to come ...

> Episode 3 ... Nota: **Now Completed 225 years later, by T.H.** ...

(As a contrast to this vision, I have annexed a fragment of a very different character, describing with equal fidelity the dream of pain and disease.--1816.)

> **... T.H. Tnkx.**

==='n thus carries on … Tariq Hameed==

. . . . Stanza 1

1.

In <u>Xanadu</u> did Kubla Khan

Lauding Wars, beyond in some unknown Sea:
Far yond Alph, where a River revered ran
Mid Folks cleaved dark, of Hearts so low of scan
Astringed: that Strangers Stranger be.

6.

Fore-warned of Errors: that Defeat did surround
For Insane Acts, goodly Intents do Ground:
As cans with holes: best efforts will not spill,
Lye ever, un-Natural rules: God's will not 'twill be;
Nature un-Natured … by Devine is set to still,
Such uncanny Pride: tumbles downwards dreary.

. . . . Stanza 2

12.

Great Kublai on Land trained, but on Ocean waned
Ô Failed planned endeavour, ships took veil never!
Hunting Holy Chanted places, shorn disgruntled
Chased by God's Winds 'n Storms dis-grunted
Wailing 'n Whining! Ends All in a Closed tower!

17.

Determined to save all, by so wreathless a cleaning,
By North by West; be it Stout, be it Sibling,
Mused off Song? Then New Rules, 'twere re-bossed:

==='n thus carries on … Tariq Hameed===

Dust thou art; returnest thee to Dust
'N when Dust werst du, wert thee ere more Frail,
A Win, a Win; never Time, never Tune, new Tale:
'N hum-birds chirp new Chants, new Force, a new Fervor
Stars Strung to Sky's Cosmos … hither 'n dither.

25.

A Winning Winner! Wins in all downed faction
Glory afore; 'n in aft, 'n in tilth 'n van,
Of clan to clan, kin to akin; skin tan to tan,
Daunt Faces! Launched Ships, in a thousandth fraction:
Drinking Chinese tea: sitting, bearing for an Hour
                    Ancestral voices prophesying war!

31.

Such a Sombre Show, in gloomed a disclosure
Question 'twas! Or Live or Die in Craves;
Singling 'n Doubling! Void of leisure
Bending bunting! Wake-up you knaves.
Wonder Stunned; all lolled: what when where's Price
Bide but by Thought: no Hurt, no Harm, nor Vice!

. . . . Stanza 3

37.

Past Mamsel in so early an ere
Lost in Lands Lost, afore 'tis that I re-saw;

=='n thus carries on ... Tariq Hameed==

Re-Lighting 'n glowing, as if of jade,
All Pure 'n clean, this Heavenly a Maid,
In Innocence Euripides' Electra.

42.

Hearing 'tis story in an open spree
Small short-story, ni brief ni long,
Nobler in Mind, a Hamlet Earthy,
Destined to play; plays Ping 'n Pong,
Founding a new Life, in Death's aware,
In Deep a Sleep: at so lame an advice!

48.

Thrice to meet again, in Times so rare,
Bear, bear; do so bear: un-flinched dare!
Cast in an Intern eye! Lo so rare, Ô rare!
Zooming Booming! Offset slice by slice,
Done Laws ... of Life or Death; well said,
As you lye Doomed in Boold too bled,
See near 'n afar, in Wise Men's guise.

54.

Evolution: Great Wars of the Great Kublai ... Third WAR ... End (Part 1) ... Deterioration & Decline

Starting from a nomadic conqueror ... of the deeps of the steppes ... to a very popular and effective ruler of a sedentary society, 'twas a remarkable transition. Ironically however, his reign witnessed not only the Mongols' most remarkable military successes, and the total subjugation of the ancient and established Song dynasty, but also 'twas miscellaneously, the most sombre and tragic of their strange and adventurous military fiascos ... Water Defeats ... multiple failed naval expeditions, against Japan, Korea, and in Vietnam and Java ... in east and in south, are historically witness assured!

♪ut B.o.k ... *thBk-E-01*9-15*.pdf-029-طارق حميد   THINKS 'n THOUGHTS -029--115-

... Tariq Hameed ... Completion & End ... Kublai Khan ...
==='n thus carries on ... Tariq Hameed==

Failed Military Campaigns

Such was the case of Naval Attacks; concerning, first Burma and after Vietnam: even successfully annexed, never covered the Costs of Annexation; remaining only as non-operant Tributary States!

Kublai also launched two failed sea-borne invasions of Japan, in 1274 & 1281. Half of a million, strong Armada in ships from China, converged off the Kyushu Island ... a **Kamikaze Typhoon**, "God Blew His Winds" ... for many Japanese "a Divine Wind", struck the fleet. Many a vessel sank! Hundreds of thousands of troops, captured or perished, or just scattered. Then, followed a failed subjugation of Java in 1293 (present-day Indonesia). Hot Tropical Heat overcame in unfriendly terrain, full of strange diseases? Not a year passed, that Kublai's forces retreated.

Kamikaze ... **Devine Wind** ... **First 1274** ... Kublai attacked with about **500** ships: Mongols conquering many Japanese settlements; but meeting fierce resistance by Samurai armies, were forced to withdraw. To avoid such mishaps in future, the Japanese prudently built two-meter-high walls all around, to avert future assaults; thus leaving No Anchoring gaps.

Second 1281 ... Kublais' **Fleet** 4,400 ships ... found No suitable Landing beach (walls): they stayed afloat for months; depleting their supplies, searching for a landing beach. Months exposure to elements ... a **Typhoon** destroyed the Fleet,

......................Then all the charm Is broken -- all that phantom-world so fair, Vanishes, and a thousand circlets spread, And each mis-shape the other. Stay awhile, Poor youth! who scarcely dar'st lift up thine eyes- The stream will soon renew its smoothness, soon The visions will return! And lo! he stays, And soon the fragments dim of lovely forms Come trembling back, unite, and now once more The **Pool becomes a Mirror**.	......................Then all the charm is sunk 'n broke -- all that random-world so rare, Vanishes, and myriads of circlets spread, For all shapes do mis-shape in time 'n while: Fool youth! who scarcely dar'st lift up thine eyes- The stream will renew its smoothness soon, soon The visions will return! And lo! he stays, And soon the fragments dim lost loving forms Come skipping back, untied, 'n vast more more That **Pool becomes a Mirror** and flan and boon.

Yet from the still surviving recollections of his mind, the Author has frequently purposed to finish for himself what had been originally, as it were, given to him ... but the to-morrow is yet to come ...

Episode 4 ... Nota: **Now Completed 225 years later, by T.H.** ...

(As a contrast to this vision, I have annexed a fragment of a very different character, describing with equal fidelity the dream of pain and disease.--1816.)

& **this tomorrow has now become**

... **T.H. Tnkx.**

=============================='n thus carries on ... Tariq Hameed==============================

....................................Stanza 1

1.

In 'tis <u>Shangtu</u> did Kublai Khan

Sensed so 'tis Age, 'tis End in a helpless plea:
Afar beyond Delph, delved where gods, to tan
Gleaning for ever 'n ever, no End no ban
Apart a few, **left** gloating in glee.

6.

Down-cast Dust! Destruct spread around
So's Crowned Horror, when Horror's Crowned:
<u>Moral:</u> Work, Work, Work; or Drill 'n Drill 'n Drill,
What'll be, 'twilled be; **in Nature, NONE can't be**;
Lone <u>Flowers</u> in **Un-till**, Decay off; just in Nil,
So shrinks ever, un-Natured: worn well scary.

....................................Stanza 2

12.

Lost or Won; Battle done's, done! Lies can't be feigned
Dreamt Power if Frails? Death prevails for ever!
'N Lifes' traces swanned be: till All be Ended
Flew what high 'n '**bove**; to finally fall a-Grounded
Clad 'tween Sobs 'n Sighs, in **dark 'n black** dower!

17.

Strength Lost but to Defeat: Ends in Stunned a-feeling,
Teaching ... **Life**'s but a Loss: Death's Dear 'Darling',
Fell, **Song**'s Might afore; hurdles many had that crossed:

==='n thus carries on ... Tariq Hameed===

Life's a creeping fuss: 'n Crumple a day, but must
To All Rose, comes a day of stale; derail de-veil,
If 'twas won, day's feat 'twas; Past 'twill Fall, 'twill Fail:
Ma Nature'll mourn! Song birds'll Sing never ever
All's but Death one day! Strikes to Fate, in a Shiver.

25.

Winners Loosers, Loosers Winners; Null negation
What can't be? Can't be: never Ending or End can,
Nor spic nor span, skin nor scope: differed race 'n scan,
Let Humans be Humans: 'n in care 'n Caution:
When Drum Sounds smite: that beat, so far be-far
                    Ancestral a voice prophesying war!

31.

Warring New, dumps Old: to Start fresh exposure
Answers New must come? Life's Not in 'Ayes';
Awake! "One's All; All's One"! Old's Gold conjecture
Lead all Roads to Heavens; thus good Done paves.
To gain Paradise just: just throw, all your Dice,
Not once, not twice; Devine Winds too, can blow thrice!

. . . . Stanza 3

37.

Wild Demoiselle of gone epoch so rare
Melodious 'n Soft: hung notes of humble bow;

=============================='n thus carries on ... Tariq Hameed=============================

Iridescenced Waters, Shimmering wade,
Leaning leanly lonesome ♪otes, somewhat delayed,
Of March Triumphal of Verdi's Aida.

42.

Arising 'Tis last 'n happy a glee
That Knew 'ner, where to belong,
ABound bl♪♪d in fl♪♪d 'n Sands Dearthy,
So Fate whiffs-off ... all in leaps 'n a prong,
That ever the Ever, in ever-bliss prepare,
For comes Oldness but once, not twice!

48.

As Fair 'tis False; 'n False 'tis Fair,
When Where's Here; 'n There's Anywhere!
Circling in a White, 'n unEnding Stair!
Doting all, to Timür: the last; the Prince,
Awaiting; that the L♪♪se End Breath, be shed,
'N downed he slept: Camp Urdu in bed,
That Spirits to the Ninth Heaven Arise.

54.

That.Spirits.to.the.Ninth.Heaven.Arise...

Beethoven's.9th.Sympohony.first.recording.(Bruno.Seidler-Winkler,1923)

Beethoven's.9th.Sympohony.(Hymn.to.Joy)...https://www.youtube.com/watch?v=nZV2EuA9fwM

... THUS ENDS TH CONTRIBUTION TO GREAT COLERIDGE'S GREAT KUBLAI KHAN ...

TH: I PREFER TO BE A TORTOISE ... NOT RABBIT   FOR A TORTOISE LIVES 500 YEARS ... NOT RABBIT ?

=='n thus carries on … Tariq Hameed==

Evolution: Great Wars of the Great Kublai … Third WAR … End Period (Part 2) … Defeat & Death

---

Death 'n Legacy … Kublai's Class System was simple … 1. Mongols: on **Top** Level
2. Central Asians: on **Middle** Level   3. Northern Chinese: on the **Low-Upper** Level …
4. Southern Chinese: on the **Low-Lower** Level … They thus, were the Highest Taxed … so in reality, in this manner, bore heaviest burden of military later defeats; suffered by **Kublai.**

His favourite wife **Chabi died in 1281**; later the oldest son in 1285: so Kublai began to withdraw from the day-to-day administration of his Empire … drinking and eating excessively, became very obese; same-way, a plaguing gout worsened: at aged 79, called to Eternity on 18th Feb 1294 … then by Customary **Ritual** 'n **Right**, was ported to the Khan's Traditional Secret Mongolian Burial Site.

Having NO heir, so succeeded by default grandson, Zhenjin's Timür; Timür lacking Kublai's diplomacy or charm, committed unpardonable errors: launching innumerable wars, at the neighbouring Muslim Rulers. Timür had a reputation, like that of "**Halaku**", of Intolerance and Mass Massacres, the typical Mongol manner: for these practices, the Mongols of later dates were labelled as pitiless **War-Mongers**! Justly, not managing to hold firm, 30 years later, earnest Uprisings began: ending the **Yuans** in the year 1368.

........................Then all the charm Is broken -- all that phantom-world so fair, Vanishes, and a thousand circlets spread, And each mis-shape the other. Stay awhile, Poor youth! who scarcely dar'st lift up thine eyes- The stream will soon renew its smoothness, soon The visions will return! And lo! he stays, And soon the fragments dim of lovely forms Come trembling back, unite, and now once more The **Pool becomes a Mirror**.	........................Then all the Charm is sunk 'n broke -- all that random-world so rare, Vanishes, and myriads of circlets spread, For all shapes do mis-shape in time 'n while: Fool youth! who scarcely dar'st lift up thine eyes- The stream will renew its smoothness soon, soon The visions will return! And lo! Aspiring he stays, And soon the fragments of dim lost loving forms Come skipping back, untied, 'n vast more more That **Pool becomes a Mirror** and flan and boon.

Yet from the still surviving recollections of his mind, the Author has frequently purposed to finish for himself what had been originally, as it were, given to him … but the to-morrow is yet to come …

Episode 5 … Nota: **Now Completed 225 years later, by T.H.** …

(As a contrast to this vision, I have annexed a fragment of a very different character, describing with equal fidelity the dream of pain and disease.--1816.)

& **this tomorrow has now become**

… T.H. Tnkx.

==='n thus carries on ... Tariq Hameed===

....Stanza 1

1.

In Xanadu did Kubla Khan

In 'tis Shangtu did Kublai Khan

In Xanadu did Kubla Khan

In 'tis Shangtu did Kublai Khan

In Xanadu did Kubla Khan

In 'tis Shangtu did Kublai Khan

2.

A stately pleasure-dome decree:

Where berged Maiden Maids with Harps in glee:

Ô Lo beheld Towers aroused to Skies yond Sea:

A day Sensed War drums, in ears eyes Presence be:

Lauding Wars, beyond in some unknown Sea:

Sensed so 'tis Age, 'tis End in a helpless plea:

3.

Where **Alph**, the sacred river, ran

Softly lo, did Saintly Spirits scan

Limpid Pools become Mirrors full plan

In Mage Images, of Strife, of Destruct 'n ban

Far yond Alph, where a River revered ran

Afar beyond Delph, delved where gods, to tan

==='n thus carries on … Tariq Hameed===

4.
Through caverns measureless to man
Thru twisted teases, Endless Gifts to van
Thru torrid whirl-p**oo**ls, of Wars cleft as can
Brothers blew Brothers, Swords slew Swords as clan
Mid Folks cleaved dark, of Hearts so low of scan
Gleaning for ever 'n ever, no End no ban

5.
Down to a sunless sea.
Away onto a Timeless spree.
As Boundless as Bounds could be.
To Sink in a deep Senseless plea.
Astringed: that Strangers Stranger be.
Apart a few, left gloating in glee.

6.
So twice five miles of fertile ground
Ran miles 'n miles of g**oo**dly downed
Stirred once mazes 'n dazes of Horrid Sound
For days in a haze of Horror Bound
Fore-warned of Errors: that Defeat did surround
Down-cast Dust! Destruct spread around

====================================='n thus carries on ... Tariq Hameed=====================================

7.

With walls and towers were girdled round
Where ups 'n downs of Fortunes un-mound:
Lost Losses 'n wins, when Battles aBound:
Lost gains Sound, when hounds go round:
For Insane Acts, goodly Intents do Ground:
So's Crowned Horror, when Horror's Crowned:

8.

And there were gardens bright with sinuous rills,
Where Flowers Sprouted, Light 'n oft, in Laughs still,
Destruct Smiles Never; or Never more'll lift or till,
Flowers petal only, where God's will's God's will,
As cans with holes: best efforts will not spill,
Moral: Work, Work, Work; or Drill 'n Drill 'n Drill,

9.

Where blossomed many an incense bearing tree;
Spring spurted in Myriad a Sense, happy to be;
But Gonged Wars a-Destined; Die or Live 'n be;
So left to Die, to Die; then good God's will 'twill be;
Lye ever, un-Natural rules: God's will not 'twill be;
What'll be, 'twilled be; in Nature, NONE can't be;

===================================='n thus carries on ... Tariq Hameed===================================

10.

And here were forests ancient as the hills,

Troubled Jungles of Past, 'twere Old to us as until,

Sad a story, Tender of Old; to Dream as will,

In forlorn Forests destroyed, oft of War's torn mill,

Nature un-Natured . . . by Devine is set to still,

Lone Flowers in Un-till, Decay off; just in Nil,

11.

Enfolding sunny spots of greenery.

Englobing Sun 'n m**oo**n: in multi-lands færie.

At Start, lots of Glory: to flatter Warlords eerie.

Thus Kings 'n Crowns fall down; tread 'n weary.

Such uncanny Pride: tumbles downwards dreary.

So shrinks ever, un-Natured: worn well scary.

. . . . Stanza 2

12.

But oh! that deep romantic chasm which slanted

Dream Charms so, Sombre faded; depth instated

Destructs Drastic, oh Sorts; in Dry Ruins Pained

Trust Failed: to Falsed Struct! All Lost, 'n Null gained

Great Kublai on Land trained, but on Ocean waned

Lost or Won; Battle done's, done! Lies can't be feigned

13.

Down the green hill athwart a cedern cover!

O'er Spaced scenes in Falls 'n Rocks, sad browns hover!

Up-Hill 'n Down-Vale, whispers 'n Revolts rover!

Ô Pain 'twas, well in vain; drawn 'Wars' rising Fever!

Ô Failed planned endeavour, ships took veil never!

Dreamt Power if Frails? Death prevails for ever!

14.

A savage place! as holy and enchanted

Magʃc Spells enlarged, Pure as 'twas dis-Chanted

Pit King 'gainst King ... brothers in arms dis-mantled

Fist to fist, face to face; Ruined 'n dis-ventured

Hunting Holy Chanted places, shorn disgruntled

'N Lifes' traces swanned be: till All be Ended

15.

As e're beneath a waning moon was haunted

Mystery bathed Mounting moon, e'er be shunted

Err's Human, in Being 'n Battle; Hope undaunted

Arc then Sword in hand, on foot on horse-back Mounted

Chased by God's Winds 'n Storms dis-grunted

Flew what high 'n 'bove; to finally fall a-Grounded

==='n thus carries on … Tariq Hameed==

16.

By woman wailing for her demon lover!

So vile Witches unveil their Demonic cover!

While, Ô wily Women; Wailed their vain endeavour!

Veiled wedded Widows, so watching their Sorts sour!

Wailing 'n Whining! Ends All in a Closed tower!

Clad 'tween Sobs 'n Sighs, in dark 'n black dower!

17.

And from this chasm, with ceaseless turmoil seething,

Unto an Abyss, with breezeless Voids a-whirling,

Lo Cry; no Rhyme nor theme! Revolts Void unmeaning,

So came once a Dream! Conquer all of all leaning,

Determined to save all, by so wreathless a cleaning,

Strength Lost but to Defeat: Ends in Stunned a-feeling,

18.

As if this earth in fast thick pants were breathing,

As Life, 'tis last ticks 'n throbs was weaning,

In throes 'n flicks so sinks the World … Reeling,

By East by South; it be Strong, it be Weakling,

By North by West; be it Stout, be it Sibling,

Teaching … Life's but a Loss: Death's Dear 'Darling',

19.

A mighty fountain momently was forced:

Lofty in disdain, momentarily was grossed:

Loosers not Choosers, in deep Thought engrossed:

Up then down, blew this Song? Unity de-crossed:

Mused off Song? Then New Rules, 'twere re-bossed:

Fell, Song's Might afore; hurdles many had that crossed:

20.

Amid whose swift half-intermitted burst

Sharp 'n Mortal, fell a fully-pungent thrust

Win or lose, or lose to win! Ends the last burst

For win's but a win; ends as Dust, or it be Crust

Dust thou art; returnest thee to Dust

Life's a creeping fuss: 'n Crumple a day, but must

21.

Huge fragments vaulted like rebounding hail,

Firm fractions flew, so reSounding Ô a Wail,

Arms, swords 'n arrows; came but to Null avail,

Nor Fail nor flail; Noise dense: Ô Cry bewail,

'N when Dust werst du, wert thee ere more Frail,

To All Rose, comes a day of stale; derail de-veil,

===================================='n thus carries on … Tariq Hameed====================================

22.

Or chaffy grain beneath the thresher's flail:

Of fluffy Pain; held on Closed pinged Lips so Frail:

Bound to be; bent to bend: no flee no ship no sail:

Conquer 'n win! Be! Stopped Null a Wind, nor Gale:

A Win, a Win; never Time, never Tune, new Tale:

If 'twas won, day's feat 'twas; Past 'twill Fall, 'twill Fail:

23.

And 'mid these dancing rocks at once and ever

Stuck 'mid these frenzied flocks, for now or never

Prisoned in shocks 'n mocks forever, in never in ever

Firm as a Rock; stiff as a Cliff: all in bevor

'N hum-birds chirp new Chants, new Force, anew Fervor

Ma Nature'll mourn! Song birds'll Sing never ever

24.

It flung up momently the sacred river.

Struggling but momentarily; down the flowing River.

Flung deep in dungy-holes; Heart 'n Soul in sever.

Surmounting but as Stars, in Firmament's Ether.

Stars Strung to Sky's Cosmos … hither 'n dither.

All's but Death one day! Strikes to Fate, in a Shiver.

==='n thus carries on ... Tariq Hameed===

25.
Five miles meandering with a mazy motion
Wonder wanders, Nature 'n Souls; of prime traction
Bent Kublai to win; to win, in swift reaction
A King Winning a Winning! Masterly action
A Winning Winner! Wins in all downed faction
Winners Loosers, Loosers Winners; Null negation

26.
Through wood and dale the sacred river ran,
In woods, Vales 'n Dells; did 'tis dusked Waters span,
In Arts 'n Craft, 'n in base 'n higher plan,
Top Artful Craft; 'n in Wars of a lofty scan,
Glory afore; 'n in aft, 'n in tilth 'n van,
What can't be? Can't be: never Ending or End can,

27.
Then reached the caverns measureless to man,
Lost 'tween breached Taverns, hues meaningful to Man,
Set unto poor 'n rich, 'n just 'n fair; as can,
Rented Breaks; in Hates 'n stakes, of Man versus Man,
Of clan to clan, kin to akin; skin tan to tan,
Nor spic nor span, skin nor scope: differed race 'n scan,

==='n thus carries on ... Tariq Hameed===

28.

And sank in tumult to a lifeless ocean:

'Tis Muse sunk in spoils, Ô so deVoid a motion:

Putting in place, Thoughts 'n Thinks; in emptive action:

Tragic Acumen of Wisdom Wise; aVoiding all faction:

Daunt Faces! Launched Ships, in a thousandth fraction:

Let Humans be Humans: 'n in care 'n Caution:

29.

And 'mid this-tumult Kubla heard from far

This hubbub during ... Kublai, hear did afar

Drum-beats; that none but Kublai heard: far so far

Pitter-a-pat; drummed Fate! Kublai eyed, away 'n far

Drinking Chinese tea: sitting, bearing for an Hour

When Drum Sounds smite: that beat, so far be-far

30.

Ancestral voices prophesying war!

Ancestral voices prophesying war!

Ancestral voices prophesying war!

Ancestral voices prophesying war!

Ancestral voices prophesying war!

Ancestral a voice prophesying war!

=================================='n thus carries on … Tariq Hameed=================================

31.

The shadow of the dome of pleasure

Rising off the Hades of the Shades of measure

Hardened Shades of Strife; nor Peace nor leisure

Shadows Shallow Strived: slitting lean a mean fissure

Such a Sombre Show, in gloomed a disclosure

Warring New, dumps Old: to Start fresh exposure

32.

Floated midway on the waves;

Bloating half-way unto the Caves;

To lye to sleep, all in their Graves;

To be or be not ? Perish Ô Slaves;

Question 'twas! Or Live or Die in Craves;

Answers New must come? Life's Not in 'Ayes';

33.

Where was heard the mingled measure

Interred 'twas a Tingled Treasure

To Dream perchance, in minced Pleasure

Dingle to Dongle! Deep in pressure

Singling 'n Doubling! Void of leisure

Awake! "One's All; All's One"! Old's Gold conjecture

 Book ... *thBk-E-01*9-15*.pdf-045- طارق حميد THINKS 'n THOUGHTS -045--115-

... Tariq Hameed ... Completion & End ... Kublai Khan ...
==='n thus carries on ... Tariq Hameed===

34.

From the fountain and the caves.
Dug in high Mounts, 'n inlaid Graves.
Dead interred be, Ô Ancient Slaves.
Sombring so: Silent in Deadly Waves.
Bending bunting! Wake-up you knaves.
Lead all Roads to Heavens; thus good Done paves.

35.

It was a miracle of rare device,
Mirages in sleep, of darkened revise,
But Kublai was Wise; 'n no fool, nor novice,
A Worldly wanderer; a-wondering thrice,
Wonder Stunned; all lolled: what when where's Price,
To gain Paradise just: just throw, all your Dice,

36.

A sunny pleasure-dome with caves of ice!
Fate's dubious Leisure-doom, Destined to slice!
Thus Chance in Life 'n Luck, threw he to Dice!
Risking, Life 'n Luck 'n Destined Chance, doubly twice!
Bide but by thought: no Hurt, no Harm, nor Vice!
Not once, not twice; Devine Winds too, can blow thrice!

....Stanza 3

37.
A damsel with a dulcimer
Floating Sad Airs, so Soft 'n fair
Knowing how to trick Lucifer
In Life so short 'n Ephemere
Past Mamsel in so early an ere
Wild Demoiselle of gone epoch so rare

38.
In a vision once I saw;
Hallucination blurred, I be-saw;
That off 'n on beamed, all but raw;
Came this brief Dream, I that fore-saw;
Lost in Lands Lost, afore 'tis that I re-saw;
Melod♪ous 'n Soft: hung ♪otes of humble bow;

39.
It was an Abyssinian maid,
'Twas 'twas of an Oriental trade,
So Dawned Light of help 'n aid,
To Softly Surely a bit did fade,
Re-Lighting 'n glowing, as if of jade,
Iridescenced Waters, Shimmering wade,

==============================='n thus carries on … Tariq Hameed==============================

40.

And on her dulcimer she played,

Dreamt ♪otes, that **no** Treason betrayed,

'N Engels' Harps, Sweetened Chants strayed,

Heavenly Mus♪c, half ♪otes inlaid,

All **Pure** 'n clean, this Heavenly a Maid,

Leaning leanly **lonesome** ♪otes, somewhat delayed,

41.

Singing of Mount Abora.

Chanting of Count Alora.

Humming of Charmed Pandora.

Delving unto E.A.Poe's Eleonora.

In Innocence Euripides' Electra.

Of March Triumphal of Verdi's Aida.

42.

Could I revive within me

Relief so strung unto me

Dawn, high Dawn; revive within me

Aye Ô Sleep! Ope hidden Eye, to History

Hearing 'tis story in an open spree

Arising 'Tis last 'n **happy** a **glee**

======================================'n thus carries on ... Tariq Hameed=======================================

43.

Her symphony and song,

Writ in ♪otes Stringed in a Throng,

Triple Destiny! Sounding 'tis gong, gong, gong,

Just to See Ending, the Dynasty Song,

Small short-story, ni brief ni long,

That Knew 'ner, where to belong,

44.

To such a deep delight 'twould win me,

Sunk in Profound Thoughts too, to rim me,

When 'tis done, 'tis done: can't undone be,

Turn full circle, Wheels; in Cries un Holy,

Nobler in Mind, a Hamlet Earthy,

A Bound blood in flood 'n Sands Dearthy,

45.

That with music loud and long,

Aye Pain in Melody, 'n in Song,

Be it a King or a Kong,

Bell Rings! Dreams un-tell! Ding 'n Dong,

Destined to play; plays Ping 'n Pong,

So Fate whiffs-off ... all in leaps 'n a prong,

==============================='n thus carries on ... Tariq Hameed==

46.

I would build that dome in air,
Bound to a Throne full of flair,
Thus Lion Lioness down laid; in theirs' lair,
Slept back unto Ma Nature's care,
Founding anew Life, in Death's aware,
That ever the Ever, in ever-bliss prepare,

47.

That sunny dome! those caves of ice!
Where Enemies Sing 'n Friends Malice!
'Twas a Lone-dome: in Fortune's 'twain Device!
Ô lo so, go to Hell ... lice, mice 'n Vice!
In Deep a Sleep: at so lame an advice!
For comes Oldness but once, not twice!

48.

And all who heard should see them there,
But who heard not, sat wither thither near,
Apart those who heard, be they anywhere,
Thunder Light or Rain, Bound 'n Bare,
Thrice to meet again, in Times so rare,
As Fair 'tis False; 'n False 'tis Fair,

===================================='n thus carries on ... Tariq Hameed====================================

49.

And all should cry, Beware! Beware!

Hearers Cries Crying Called! Aware! Beware!

Here There, or in the After-Where!

So be discrete, try not to stare!

Bear, bear; do so bear: un-flinched dare!

When Where's Here; 'n There's Anywhere!

50.

His flashing eyes, his floating hair!

Eyes all did smash, in gloat 'n in blare!

Ô Courage aBound, be fair to be-fair!

Vacant: in Pensive moods ... sharped Eclair!

Cast in an Intern eye! Lo so rare, Ô rare!

Circling in a White, 'n unending Stair!

51.

Weave a circle round him thrice,

In Magic circles, wove once twice thrice,

Round go Mysteries, where Phantoms do slice,

Struck Lone, by Fortune's Magic Dice,

Zooming Booming! Off-set slice by slice,

Doting all, to Timür: the last; the Prince,

===================================='n thus carries on ... Tariq Hameed===

52.

And close your eyes with holy dread,

Firm Blank Open eyes, unHoly Dead,

Darkened fixed gaze, NO Thoughts in 'tis head,

Never to awake: in bed or in spread,

Done Laws ... of Life or Death; well said,

Awaiting; that the L**oo**se End Breath, be shed,

53.

For he on honey-dew hath fed,

L**oo**se honeyed dews, which never spread,

Gone with the Wind; in Death's g**oo**d Old Wed,

Where bells tolled in a dark cold shed,

As you lye D**oo**med in B**oo**ld t**oo** bled,

'N downed he slept: Camp Urdu in bed,

54.

And drunk the milk of Paradise.

Hark, Ô milks 'n brews which Ecstasise.

That, Paradise or Hell be any-Wise.

To Wisely our History to revise.

See near 'n afar, in Wise-Men's guise.

That Spirits to the Ninth Heaven Arise.

==========================='n thus carries on ... Tariq Hameed===============================

That Spirits to.the.Ninth.Heaven.Arise...   Beethoven's.9th.Sympohony.first.recording.(Bruno.Seidler-Winkler,1923)

Beethoven's.9th.Sympohony.(Hymn.to.Joy)...https://www.youtube.com/watch?v=nZV2EuA9fwM

.......................Then all the charm Is broken -- all that phantom-world so fair, Vanishes, and a thousand circlets spread, And each mis-shape the other. Stay awhile, Poor youth! who scarcely dar'st lift up thine eyes- The stream will soon renew its smoothness, soon The visions will return! And lo! he stays, And soon the fragments dim of lovely forms Come trembling back, unite, and now once more The **Pool becomes a Mirror**.	.......................Then all the *Charm* is sunk 'n broke -- all that random-world so rare, Vanishes, and myriads of circlets spread, For all shapes do mis-shape in time 'n while: Fool youth! who scarcely dar'st lift up thine eyes- The stream will renew its smoothness soon, soon The visions will return! And lo! Aspiring he stays, And soon the fragments of dim lost loving forms Come skipping back, untied, 'n vast more more That **Pool becomes a Mirror** and flan and boon.

Initial Upbringing … Life, in the First Steppes

Kublai Khan … famous Genghis' grandson, history's Great Conqueror! Childhood's shortly documented; with minimal bare facts. Born 23 September 1215, to Tolui (4th. and youngest son of Genghis), mother Sorkhotani, princess of Kereyid Confederacy: Tolui's politically influential mother, set him goals of leadership: compete with cousins & uncles, ruling Mongol Empire. Sorkhotani … as described by Rashid ud-Din of Persia, was "extremely intelligent & able, towering above all the women in the world". Ögödei, his elder suffered a severe illness: Tolui volunteered sacrifice; & died consuming a cursed drink.

Sorkhotani's legendary political savvy for Kublai & his brothers, including Hulagu, went towards control of Mongol's Domains. Kublai, since early childhood, was an expert of traditional Mongol Arts, excelling in all sports; he relished the hunt all his life … which served him fairly well in war and conquests in later life.

The most prominent and influential element of his early years, was his study and strong attraction for the existing Chinese Culture. He thus requested **Haiyun**, a Northern Chinese Buddhist Monk of **Shangtu**, to his Mongolian **Urdu** (Camp). Meeting Haiyun in 1243 in Karakorum, he introduced Kublai to Buddhist Philosophy. Later 'twas Haiyun who then introduced the former Daoist, become now a Buddhist Monk, Liu **Bingzhong**: Painter, Calligrapher, Poet, Mathematician, he soon took charge as Kublai's new Advisor. Kublai often employed people of foreign origins, as he was earnestly bent to amalgam all interests: **Local**, **Mongol**, and **Turk**, to the **Betterment** of **Imperial** needs.

Secondary Steps … from the Steppes, to the Steeps … Xanadu

As successful campaigns had greatly expanded Kublai's Domain, Time was to gain Concern of Chinese Clans, by a **New Capital**; Kublai ordered advisors to Select a Site, *feng shui* rules acted (**Harmony**): a mid-way area 'tween China's Agricultural Space & Mongolian Steppe. This, New Northern Capital was initially Named **Shang-tu**, (*Upper Capital*: in contrast of **Chung-tu**, *Central Capital*, by now Beijing). Europeans travellers later, pronounced it, as **Xanadu**.

==='n thus carries on ... Tariq Hameed===

Kublai's Rise to Greatness … and Winning of the Ultimate Supreme Power

Primary Conquests in China

At start, Kublai was exerting full power on most **Eurasia**; but, opponents to Mongol rule were holding still hands behind back … Thus Kublai needed conquering southern China; a do or die effort …
Object … Uniting China.

Then happens, the climactic battle at Karakoram: where Arik Boké's armies, a crushing defeat suffer; attacked by the surprising Kublai. The younger's forces surrendered not! However, soon in August of 1264, Arik Boké admitted defeat … Finally deposing arms in **Shangtu** City.

Kublai now undisputed, then started to reign, as the Great Khan: all Mongolia, as well as the mostly Mongol-occupied China, not only became a very wider but also a much looser empire … the Ilkhanate exactly in the Middle and a powerful Russian **Golden.Horde**, supporting. Because of the vastness of his Domains, Kublai could NEVER feel secure; that his real hold, on the Song China was dubious, not sure … in counter, he kept his total attention, ever and ever Southward.

Thus little by little, the Great Khan directly came to control the Mongol Homeland and all possessions in China. Heading the largest Mongol Empire ever, with powerful authority over all the leaders of the **Golden.Horde** in old Russia, including the Ilkhanate, of the then Middle East; thus many other hordes, came also under his total control.

Song China Conquest

Winning so, the Chinese hearts and minds was then of primordial importance to Kublai Khan … some maintaining that he converted to Buddhism, moving his Capital to Dadu (today's Peking or **Beijing**); renaming his own dynasty, as *Dai Yuan* in 1271. Naturally, abandoning his Mongol and Islamic heritage, could have sparkled violent riots in Karakoram … ***however, such affirmations seem to be biased***?

These tactics nevertheless were successful. Most Imperial **Song** Family surrendered formally to Kublai Khan in 1276; their Royal seal so was yielded, but the resistance did not end … Empress Dowager, led the Loyalists until 1279, when at the Yamen Battle, the **Song** China finally accepted their defeat. Eventually, the palace was surrounded by the Mongol forces; when a Song official, holding just a young 8-year-old Chinese Emperor jumped into the ocean: thus drowning both … such was their **L**oyalty, to their **R**oyalty! So did Kublai Master **China** and the **Golden.Horde**.

Disambiguation: Ulug Ulus "Great State", a Khanate created in the 13th. century, became functionally separated in 1259, as **Kipchak** (Ulus of Jochi) Khanate. When it's Founder, Batu Khan died in 1255, his dynasty kept on flourishing for another hundred year (1359), despite internal disputes. Adopting Islam, **Uzbeg Khan** ruled from 1312 to 1341 … really at peak-time, he extended to unknown spans afore!

In West … from Siberia (Central Asia) to Eastern Europe, and from the Urals to the Danube …
In South … from the **Black** to the **Caspian** Seas, bordering **Caucasian** Mountains (already conquered Territories of the Mongol dynasty included) … those which were popularly known as the **Ilkhinates**.

===================================='n thus carries on ... Tariq Hameed====================================

The Yuan Dynasty of China, c. 1294

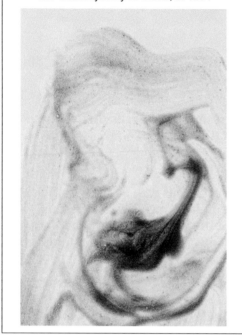

Golden.Horde

https://www.pexels.com/search/golden%20dragon/

pexels-photo-4046718.jpeg

Golden.Horde, comes from Russian or Turkish sources, inspired by the golden colour of **Mongol Wartime Tents**, representing the great wealth of Batu Khan (son of Jochi, eldest son of **Genghis**).

The **Mongol** (and Turkish) word **Urdu** means
"**Camp**" or "**Palace**",

Term "**Golden.Horde**" became popular in 16th. century, to designate a particular successor of the Mongol Khanate.

Golden.Horde, Blue Horde, White Horde
seems unused, by Mongols.

Its 1st. use, applied to Batu, centred in Sarai.

Conquer ... Conquer ... and ... Conquer ... and ... Conquer

Kublai Khan as Yuan Emperor

Though Kublai Khan obtained power by arms, his reign featured notable advances in political structures, as much as in known sciences and arts. This first Yuan Emperor's bureaucracy was founded on purely traditional **Mongol Urdu System**, but Kublai accepted a number of traditional Chinese administrative practices.

Kublai had a few tens of thousands of Mongols, to rule Chinese millions: so the Kublai Khan engaged a heavy quantity of original and competent traditional Chinese advisors, devisers, administrators and officials.

Flourished artistic new styles; as set in a melding pot of Tibetan and Chinese Buddhism: issuing gold reserve backed **paper currency**, valid all through China; also patronizing **clockmakers** and **astronomers**: and even hiring a Chinese Monk ... to create a **script** for Western China's languages, till yet non-literate.

NOTA: 'Tis said, that the Chinese were the first to devise a system of paper money, in approximately **770 B.C.**

Inexpensive Paper of **Natural Fibres**, made **Paper Money** possible ...

thus metals anew found their customary use. Empire Distant Lands, so were favoured (cause Transferable)!

1st. Town **Szechuan** ... Themes: **Houses, Trees, Humans!**

======================================='n thus carries on … Tariq Hameed=======================================

Kublai Khan as Adventurer

Kublai Khan … **Unchallenged Ruler** of the Richest and Largest World Empire? But, to control his warlike nature couldn't remain silent infinitely. Restless, he looked East; managing to penetrate much Asian Southeast: Burma and part of Vietnam … Conquests Costly …

All Expense, Null Return, Profitless Ventures.

Master of Land, Miserable on sea **… 'Tween 1274 and 1293, he finally attempted to invade Japan and conquer Java … bringing the Great Khan new unwelcome experiences:** Military Failure**. His fleet was stormed by Japanese Tempests, named in Japan** "kamikaze" **… the** "Devine Winds" **… The** Sunk Armada! **These defeats seemed to most of his subjects,**

that 'twas like a sign that he had lost the "Mandate of Heavens"**?**

Marco Polo Visit

For Europeans, Marco Polo's long visit, with father and uncle was **Historical**: for Mongols, 'twas only a **Footnote**? Visiting afore in 1271, the elders delivered the Pope's letter; and Oil from Jerusalem to Kublai. Gifted in languages, the 16-year-old Marco accompanied his elders … the Venetian Merchants.

After 3½ years journey, the Polos reached **Shangtu**. Marco served as a minor functionary, in the court; Kublai Khan denied several times, the family's return request to Venice. The return took two years, from 1292.

Parting with a wedding cortege, that included a Mongol princess to marry in Persia an Ilkhan prince. Sailing the Indian Ocean Trade Route, introduced Marco Polo, to actual Vietnam, Malaysia, Indonesia and India. The young Marco's vivid descriptions of Asian travels and experiences, narrated to a close friend, inspired so many another European later, to seek wealth in the exotic Far East. But, we tend ever to over-rate Marco's influence! Remember: traditional trade along the Silk Road was in full flow, long before Polo's travelogue was published.

Kublai Khan's Invasions and Blunders

Though ruling the world's richest empire in Yuan China, as well as the second-largest land empire that ever existed in modern history, the Khan was discontent. He grew more and more obsessed, with further conquest; in East and Southeast Asia.

European Recollections of Kublai arc … **Barbarian Civilised**, Mongol become Chinese; Distant *Time 'n Space Monster* suddenly doting Habits of a Distinguished 'n Refined Monarch: cause an imminent Disaster from the East had come, *a short few days' ride, **off the Atlantic Ocean** …*
The Inborn **Nightmare** of the **West**, to be **Dominated** by the **East** … **Chaos Averted**!

But to the South-East **Asians' Eyes**, Up 'n Northwards; a China Immense Overhanging and Present … **Kublai** was a Man of many a Pronged Planning, to Conquer the South-East of Asia … Not Remote Materialized, but a **True Threat Actual**, of Momentous Depth Changes … **But Remain** …

European Fears … a Fully Integral a part, of the **present-day World Topicality**.

Kublai Gone: closed China to Classical Bounds. "**He Who Laughs, Lasts**", but … Peace 'n Sun Rise in East!

Future Reveals **NEVER** 'tis Secrets afore 'tis Time … Silk **Belt is Road: 'n the Road is Belt**?

==================================='n thus carries on ... Tariq Hameed==

Decline and Death

Death of the Great Khan

Kublai's favourite wife and his closest companion, Chabi died in 1281: followed closely in 1285 by another sad event, the death of Zhenjin; Kublai's heir apparent and the oldest son. Suffering closely, such enormous personal losses, our Great Khan began slowly to withdraw totally from his own Empire's administration.

Kublai tried to drown his sorrow, digging deep into alcohol and luxurious food. He had previously been subjected to gout (inflammatory disease), which worsened; growing quite obese. After a long decline, Kublai finally passed away on the 18th. Feb 1294: to be buried as usage, in the **Khans'** Mongolian Secret Burial Place.

blai Khan's Legacy

The Great Khan was succeeded by his grandson, Timür Khan, son of Zhenjin. His daughter, Khutugh-beki, who married King Chungnyeol of Goryeo (Korea): thus becoming the Queen of Korea, simultaneously.

After centuries of strife, struggle, division, Kublai Khan finally re-united China. Nevertheless, that his founded Dynasty **Yuan** was overthrown in 1368, 'tis notable, that it set a precedent for future: Manchu **Qing** Dynasty.

Genghis Khan Cavalry Tactics

1. **Lightning Cavalry**: No Reins, No Saddle; only Knee Control ... 2 Sheaths, 1 **Bow**, 2 Swords
2. **Double Arched Bow**: Hand Hold, then Top & Low Arcs ... 2 Outer **Wood**; with Inlaid **Steel**
3. **Hard Tungsten Arrow-Head**: Could Pierce any Armour ... in **Rapid** Range of 200 meters
4. **2nd. Phase Attack**: Once Empty, Sheaths were Thrown ... Double **Swords** Continued Attack

Kublai Khan Diplomatic Ability

1. **Lightning Cavalry**: As **Genghis** ... However, Kublai Converts Horsemen to Sailor-Marines
2. **Modern Muslim Technology**: Adapted **Saladin Catapults**, to Storm 'n Stone Castle Walls
3. **Despot by Birth, but Clement by Policy**: Pardoned Many of the Conquered, unto Partner
4. **His Grand Lady Chabi**: Taught Court Princesses,, Weave Used Bow-Strings to Warm-Robes

Reference Sources:

- Polo, Marco, Hugh Murray & Giovanni Battista Baldelli Boni.

   The Travels of Marco Polo, New York: Harper & Brothers, 1845.

   The Kubla Khan Manuscript and its First ... – Jstor   www.jstor.org › stable

by H KELLIHER · 1994 · Cited — Coleridge's **Kubla Khan, Or A Vision in a Dream**, first **printed** with ... The Pains of Sleep in 1816! There followed a silence of three months **before** he returned to this topic ... Childers (**London, 1925**).

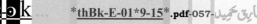

================================'n thus carries on ... Tariq Hameed===============================

Kublai Khan ... the Mongol Emperor of China ... Method of Gathering Immense Power

Mongol Empire at its highest peak! The largest Empire, world ever saw! Grandson of Genghis, Kublai Khan (1215-1294), followed his elder's policy of Militarized Conquest.

However, he always advised good-sense altruism and practiced the development of arts and sciences. Founder of Yuan Dynasty, took over as Chinese Emperor. Ögödei Khan, his uncle, in 1236, granted him 10,000 household fiefdom, in North China's Hebei Province ... but Kublai, let his Mongol Agents complete autonomy, who exaggerated with Taxes, that large number of peasants quit ... thus forcing Kublai to directly halt mistrust ... this wise policy, returned much of the population; that Sanity Reigned!

Möngké, Kublai's brother, becoming the Great Khan, named him the Northern Viceroy. Kublai, well attached to Chinese Traditions, found it better to select a New Capital. Thus was found a Compromise ... a terrain 'tween the Mongolian Steppes and typical Agricultural Panorama of Old China ... the Upper Capital (Shangtu), which was later Europeanised, as Xanadu! This slowly became, at first Peking: then today's Beijing!

In 1259, Möngké died, while Kublai was in war in Sichuan. Kublai, had the foresight, of not to abandon this war; so allowing his brother Arik Boké, to convene an assembly of Mongolian and Turkish Lords (Kuriltai), in the Capital City of Karakoram. Here Boké was named the new Great **Khan**: which was totally negated by Kublai and by his brother Hulagu: both then called another 'Kurital', which named Kublai, the new Global Khan ...

started so several long Civil Wars.

Chronology of Events ... 1251 to 1294 ... Span of Kublai Life History		
Birth ... 23 September 1215	Death ... 18 February 1294	Dadu Khanbaliq (Beijing) ... Aged **79**
Reign ... 5/5/1260 to 18/2/1294	Nationality ... Mongolian	Dynasty Newly Founded ... **Yuan**
Coronation ... 5 May 1260	Predecessor ... Möngké Khan	Successor ... Timür (Zhenjin) Khan
Consorts (Khatun): Tegulen, Qoruqchin, **Chabi**, Dorbajin, Hushijin, Bayujin, Nambui (Chabi's Consent, at Death)		

Chabi ... Khatun (Wife) of Kublai : Active Empress of the Mongol Empire

A Mongol princess **Chabi**, a remarkable woman? Was the third & favourite wife of Kublai.

Other than his mother, no other woman held such a prominent position in the Yuan Empire as Chabi did and, like the mother of Kublai (a Nestorian Christian), her influence was especially felt in dealing with religion. Chabi, was a devout Tibetan Buddhist, through whom Buddhism became very prominent, in the Yuan Dynasty period. She practised an

=='n thus carries on ... Tariq Hameed==

absolute Religious Freedom. She also exemplified a smooth power transition, towards the defeated dynasty **Song**: treating them with their due Hon ur, Dig ty and Res ect.

Practical and efficient, she set new styles of brimmed-wide sleeveless tunics for Mongol troops, in the warmer southern climates; different to frozen Mongol Steppes. She was of nomadic tribes: so she maintained "**Efficiency in Scarcity**". She taught Court Ladies to Spin used Bow Strings to cloth ... NOT that they go waste. Kublai Khan at her death in 1281, NEVER was same again, often depressed: eventually led to his death (1294)! There is enough historical evidence, to affirm, that it was due to Excessive Food!

Legacy of Kublai Khan

Celebrated above most of the Chinese Emperors, Kublai helped forming the political traditions, in alike way, of his own Mongols. A revered adviser, the Tibetan Grand-Lama Phang-pa, developed a historical Political Theory, "**Dual Principle**"… in other words … "**1: Power Parity 2: Religious Dig ty … 3: In Political State**".
A Theory of **Practical Effect**: on later history? See 1911: Theocratic Monarchy Liberating Mongolia from China.
The real **Kublai** is very difficult to assess. In a panegyric, rather an un-sober appraisal, Marco Polo sees Kublai as an ideal universal sovereign; he largely ignored his human weaknesses; feast and hunt indulgence, and failure in exercising supervision properly over subordinates; against occasional cruelty outbursts.

Kublai had dual roles: **1.** As traditional type Chinese Emperor, he was not able to resolve the inherent contradictions, of mixed traditions; finally failing to **Reconcile the Opposites**: even ruling with the added advantage of unfettered absolutism, a key-point of the ancient apparatus of historical China! **2.** Of a man of unlimited will-power energy and vision unto political insight; he finally, just ended-up into a defunct schema. Of exclusion of his Mongol homeland, China absorbed his interests and his energies, for many a many a year; self-engaging in civil-wars against his rival Mongol Steppes-Princes. His policies isolated Mongols in China, from their own environment. Under him, of course Mongols privileged, enjoyed many a brilliant prosperity spells: later this politics was pursued less skilfully, by successors. So, 30 years after him, very serious uprisings occurred against the remaining Mongols: with the final dynasty collapse in 1368. Then, Mongols withdrawing to their old Steppes, played just a minor role: only of their own local importance.

Kublai's Successor ... Timür

Earlier Aspect: Kublai entrusted the Golden Horde's Revision of the 2nd. Census to **Timür** (Zhenjin) Khan; his **Object**: was a substantial Provision of Material Resources and Armies: for his ultimate desire; Conquest of Northern China ...
Later Aspect: Mongol regime in China, was renamed **Dai Yuan** in 1271: for he sought to Sinicize his own image as the sole Emperor of China … in a bid to win over Control of the Han Chinese Clans, who were Counted in Millions.

Timür Khan ran the empire as Kublai Khan, with few economic reforms; his glory never was great: recover a finance bled by the expensive campaigns of Vietnam … People of different origins, **Mongols**, **Han** Chinese, **Muslims**, few **Christians**, formed the **Highest Posts of Empire**. Peace was declared in last years, 'tween Yuans and Mongols, but 'twas not for long. In his final spell, his only son Teshou, died a year earlier … then later, Timür passed-off on 10th. February 1307: without heir.

(**Nota**: Not to Confuse …**Timerlane**, Timür Lang; the Limper, was born in **1336**).

=='n thus carries on ... Tariq Hameed==

Great Wars of the Great Kublai ... The Youthful ... Early Period ... Afore Ilkhanate

Ilkhan means **Viceroy**, title of *Hulagu* son of Tolui, *grandson* of Genghis, younger *brother* of Möngké: third brother being **Kublai**, the so Great Mongol Khan (1260-1294), who later controlled the post **Song** North China. Hulagu ... ordered to administer full Mongol rule over then **West Asia**, from 1253 CE, mobilised to expand to Iran and Iraq; crushed the ruling Ismailites (named "**Assassins**", originally "**Hashish** Sellers". Abbasid Caliph (**adoring Diamonds**), collapsed by Hulagu: rapid capture of Baghdad. Executing the Caliph (**eat Gems**), a week-long slaughter Killed 800,000, per tradition; immense a Syrian Massacre followed: "**Halaku**" now synonym of "Killer" ... is common coin in Urdu!

This Name still lingers on in "Urdu": Pakistan and India ... instituted in Mongol/Mughal Rule (**1526 to 1857**).

By end decade, Mongols divided into three distinct Khanates, ruled by many branches of Genghis' successors: generally named **Ilkhantes** ... **Chagatai Khanate**, Golden.Horde; and lastly, the **Yuan Dynasty**, of the Great Kublai Khan!

Kublai as young, lived in a Round Tent, named "**Yurt**" ... (Urdu Genghis). Who were the **Mongols**?

Originated by Unification of Nomadic Clans: from many diverse regions of the then Central Mongolia. When Kublai was born, Genghis' Empire, extended, from a **Sea Caspian** to an **Ocean Pacific**: conquering Yen-Ching (Beijing)! Thus, when his uncle Ögödei became the Great Khan, he trusted Kublai a fiefdom of about 10,000 households, which he administered by proxy ... but soon directly ... realising the injustice Imposed by the Imposed Rulers!

Episode 1 ... https://www.pexels.com/search/Beijing/ ... www.pexels.com/photo/great-wall-of-china-2412603/

==='n thus carries on ... Tariq Hameed===

Great Wars of the Great Kublai … First WAR … Middle Period (Part 1) … The Ilkhanate

At Genghis' advice, Sorkhotani chose a Buddhist woman as Kublai's nurse. Genghis Khan also performed a ritual for his first hunt at nine years old, when he Killed a rabbit and an antelope; smearing per the Mongol customs, the animal's fat, on the mid finger: saying "All Ye! **Heed the words of this young boy**; so full of wisdom". Genghis died! Kublai's father Tolui served for a couple of years as regent; then his uncle Ögödei was enthroned. When Mongols conquered the **Jins**, Ögödei gifted Kublai his own estate. However inexperienced, he reigned by proxy; corruption resulted by an ingrained and **self-help**, '**put in pocket**' official's excessive taxation: huge Chinese peasants' flocks flight; resulting in Tax losses! Kublai wisely intervening rapidly, reformed with newer officials, helping the previously fled peasants, to return.

Kublai since the early years, was greatly amorous of Chinese Art and Culture; so invited a prominent Buddhist monk, Haiyun to his Mongol "**Urdu**" (Camp) ... Kublai's always Wise and Sage endeavours, to '**Balance the Opposites**', engaged diverse Nationalities … respectfully: *Buddhist, Christens and Muslims*.

Ordered in 1253 attacking Yunnan, he requested submission. Ruling, Dali-Gao family murdered his team. The Mongol East Wing went to Sichuan Basin: West Wing to West Sichuan: and Kublai went over southern grasslands, to take the capital city of **Dali** (Old Tali: Yunnan): strangely & wisely, he spared the residents, his envoy's slayers. The Dali King defected, surrendering the use of his forces … Wisely, Duan Xingzhi, last Dali King, was named local ruler (**Tusi**); a pacification officer also appointed … Peace, Ô Peace, lasted not long? **Kublai departed and Trouble broke**! Unrest arose 'mongst certain factions. However, Xingzhi pacified the court; offering Möngké detail maps of Yunnan: and likewise counselled on the methodology of the vanquishing of the resisting tribes ... and he also furnishing the Mongol army, many guides, deploys and vanguards. Before end 1256, Uryankhadai's armies had pacified Yunnan.

https://www.pexels.com/search/Beijing/ … https://www.pexels.com/photo/multicolored-concrete-building-with-a-lake-view-showing-the-distinct-architectural-design-of-ancient-china-2846005/ … Episode 2 …

==='n thus carries on ... Tariq Hameed===

Great Wars of the Great Kublai … Second WAR … Middle Period (Part 2) … Song Conquest

Kublai Khan: first Mongol to transform Mongol horsemen, as efficient and solid naval force, played a decisive role in the famous battle of Xiangyang (1267-73) … turning-point in Mongol's long war against an established **Song** Dynasty's centuries old rule over China. All started in 1265, after Möngké's decade long but totally unsuccessful campaign against the **Songs**; where Kublai captured 146 **Song** warships in Sichuan battle. This early victory gave him the nucleus of his Mongol fleet. Kublai recognized quickly, that it was of vitally a great importance, mastering **Song's** riverine superiority … to quote a well-known ancient dictum, **"If 'twere existed no Yangtze River, 'twere be NO Songs existing!"** … traditions age-old, the Mongol armies were best known for their able horse-back agility … but Kublai's navy, furnished the formal blow: subjugating traditional China.

At outset, Kublai faced a dilemma insoluble, vividly expressed by a strong memorial by a Wisely Wise, old Chinese Sage, **"I have heard, one can conquer an empire on horseback, but can one govern it on horseback?"** China was impossible, administered by Mongols inexperienced … Adoption of existing Chinese methods & patterns was obliged. That 'twas done to full extent, assuredly & slowly; retake established procedures: to extent of losing their personal identity. However, working through Chinese agents, they avoided to be alienated from the population masses; which could have rejected them at any moment (and that's what exactly happened later, in 1368).

The Mongols, numerically inferior, used to different patterns of life and less advanced culturally than Chinese, just **could not rule China for long, as a privileged distinct caste**. So, Kublai's historical personal decision was brilliant.

Episode 3 … https://www.pexels.com/search/Beijing/ … www.pexels.com/photo/city-art-building-roof-6339175/

==='n thus carries on ... Tariq Hameed==

Great Wars of the Great Kublai ... Third WAR ... End Period (Part 1) ... Deterioration & Decline

Starting from a nomadic conqueror ... of the deeps of the steppes ... to a very popular and effective ruler of a sedentary society, 'twas a remarkable transition. Ironically however, his reign witnessed not only the Mongols' most remarkable military successes, and the total subjugation of the ancient and established Song dynasty, but also 'twas miscellaneously, the most sombre and tragic of their strange and adventurous military fiascos ... Water Defeats ... multiple failed naval expeditions, against Japan, Korea, and in Vietnam and Java ... in east and in south, are historically witness assured!

Failed Military Campaigns ...

Such was the case of Naval Attacks; concerning, first Burma and after Vietnam: even successfully annexed, never covered the Costs of Annexation; remaining only as non-operant Tributary States!

Kublai also launched two failed sea-borne invasions of Japan, in 1274 & 1281. Half of a million, strong Armada in ships from China, converged off the Kyushu Island ... a **Kamikaze Typhoon**, "God Blew His Winds" ... for many Japanese "a Divine Wind", struck the fleet. Many a vessel sank! Hundreds of thousands of troops, captured or perished, or just scattered. Then, followed a failed subjugation of Java in 1293 (present-day Indonesia). Hot Tropical Heat overcame in unfriendly terrain, full of strange diseases? Not a year passed, that Kublai's forces retreated.

Episode 4 ... https://www.pexels.com/search/Beijing/ ... www.pexels.com/photo/people-riding-on-boat-2845970/

==='n thus carries on ... Tariq Hameed==

Great Wars of the Great Kublai … Third WAR … End Period (Part 2) … Defeat & Death

Death 'n Legacy

Kublai's Class System was simple:

1. Mongols: on **Top** Level
2. Central Asians: on **Middle** Level
3. Northern Chinese:
   on the **Low-Upper** Level …
4. Southern Chinese:
   on the **Low-Lower** Level …

They thus, were the Highest Taxed **…** so in reality, in this manner, bore heaviest burden of military later defeats; suffered by **Kublai.**

His favourite wife **Chabi died in 1281**; later the oldest son in 1285: so Kublai began to withdraw from the day-to-day administration of his Empire … drinking and eating excessively, became very obese; same-way, a plaguing gout worsened: at aged 79, called to Eternity on 18th Feb 1294 … then by Customary **Ritual** 'n **Right**, was ported to the Khan's Traditional Secret Mongolian Burial Site.

Having NO heir, so succeeded by default grandson, Zhenjin's Timür; Timür lacking Kublai's diplomacy or charm, committed unpardonable errors: launching innumerable wars, at the neighbouring Muslim Rulers.

Timür had a reputation, like that of "**Halaku**", of Intolerance and Mass Massacres, the typical Mongol manner: for these practices, the Mongols of later dates were labelled as pitiless **War-Mongers**! Justly, not managing to hold firm, 30 years later, earnest Uprisings began: ending the **Yuans** in the year 1368.

Episode 5 … https://www.pexels.com/search/Beijing/ … www.pexels.com/photo/light-city-people-street-6339182/

==='n thus carries on ... Tariq Hameed===

Religion and the Great Kublai ... Tolerance ... Concerning ... Christianity, Buddhism & Islam

---

Kublai **encouraged** all types of Asian Arts and Cultures ... He also had an enormous tolerance, for all sorts of Religions.

Christianity ...

Kublai's mother, Sorkhotani was a Nestorian Christian!

Mongols, primarily Nomads, practiced religion in **Acts**, **Not Rituals** (The Normally Accepted Western Way). No Churches or Monasteries, but **Beliefs Practiced**! Jesus, a Healer (considered Shaman) **Respect Interwove** ... **1.** Curing Sick: **2.** Christian **Cross**, as pointed all four directions, was **Universality**: **3.** Eating Meat, affirmed them **Nomads**; Not vegetarian Buddhists: **4.** Hard-drinking, they appreciated **alcohol**, as valid Church Service: **5.** And Last, but Not the Least ... the Name **Jesus**! Sounding *Yesu*, the Sacred Number "9" for the Mongols ... Strangely, 'twas also the name of Genghis' father, **Yesugei**. Once even a Trade Silk-Route Pact with the Pope was settled! History notes: Pope tried allying them ... Warring Muslim Mamelukes: to **Hold over Holy-Lands**!

Buddhism ...

In Ancient Mongolia, Buddhism introduced itself in 2 Waves!

Mongols, primarily Nomads, were subjected to 2 distinct Buddhist insertions ... of **Ashoka** and **Genghis** ...
1st. Wave: Cave Paintings demonstrate ... that in the 3rd. BC, Indian Emperor Ashoka extended his domain to the North, engaging into the Trade of the Silk-Route, widely profitable; capturing Khotan, in Hor; as per Lobsang, inclusive part of Mongolia! By tradition, Mongolian Lama, is Zaya Pinda; incarnation of Ashoka!

2nd. Wave: Genghis adopted Sakya Buddhism (Tibetan) ... Kublai promoted his Guru, Papka-Lama, inventing a new Script, named "**Pakyig**": the official vehicle of notices, communications and governmental regulations. Learned Buddhists, when moderate, were in good esteem ... However, whether Kublai, basically a Muslim, changed? **History Negates** ... since one of his elders (**Birkai**) adopted Islam; also his successors, like Timür, even if he deviated in religious practice, or declared war on Mamelukes and others: remained firmly Muslim!

Islam and Muslims ...

Birkai 1st. Muslim Khan of the Golden.Horde (1257 to 1266)

Islamic Scholars: Thrived notable figures as Nasir ud-din al-Tusi, with numerable astronomical discoveries. He promoted **Muslim** Scholars, Astronomers, Military and Civil Scientists, to institute Observatories, creating newer and efficient Instruments of Measure: that which allowed even the Correction of the Chinese Calendar!

The Bureau of **Islamic Astronomy** in Xanadu, was founded by Kublai Khan, under Jamal-ud-din. Survive no records, but data is Re-Constructible from Old Persian, Arabic and other remaining Chinese documents.

In North China, 1000 km over Beijing, exist today, **Mosques of Kublai Epoch** ... with **Qura'anic** Verses!

==='n thus carries on ... Tariq Hameed==

Mongols, primarily Nomads, had a feeble for **Muslims** ... The first Muslim Khans being **Birkai** & **Ghazan**, later generations followed suite: in any case making Concessions, as per Needs of the Day ... as per all Rulers.

1. In **8** of the **12** Districts of China, over **30** Muslims were engaged in Kublai's Court as the Highest Officials ... **Shams-ud-din Omar** (Yunnan Governor): Muhammad **Yalavach** (<u>Xanadu</u>'s **Mayor**)!
2. Muslim Physicians had self-created their own Clinics & Hospitals ... to largely serve the Public! The Medicine Institute <u>Xanadu</u> "Extensive Mercy Dept.", was renowned in Surgery & Medicine!
3. Surprisingly, the works of famous **Bu-Ali-Sena** (Avicenna) were also published, in same period!
4. Accurate Cartography by Muslims, the long of the **Silk-Route**, allowed **Mapping** of total China!
5. **Up-Step**: Muslim Mathematics: Euclidian Geometry: Spherical Trigonometry: Arabic Numerals!
6. **And Toping it All**: re-Inventing **Muslim Trebuchet** (Wooden Catapult): to Conquer Xiangyang!

A Note on the Historical Evidence ... Maximum care has been employed to avoid any Bias or Prejudice, in the Historical Events ... which have been accumulated through Diverse Sources in Time ... **They have been abridged** and completely molded into my own Idiom, of other date: respecting the mighty 'n **poetical language**, of **Coleridge** ... Muslim or Buddhist? Lyes Where <u>Truth</u> ?

A Strange Historical Miracle ... Advent of Paper Currency ... in Ancient and Kublai's China

Tangs 800 on, invented paper money, the "**Flying Cash**", as it **Flew** away when **Wind Blew**. However, in August 1260, Kublai himself, initiated the first official unified paper currency ... unto the large and span of the Yuan Empire. It was named **Chao**, with **NUL expiry date**. This convertible currency, to Gold and Silver, was acceptable for the Government's Tax Payments, thus becoming a security against any type of loss or devaluation: for conquest of the **Song**, Kublai issued a newer type of State Sponsored paper note ... but it crashed ... as a total economic failure. So, **Kublai** was the **World's first "Fiat Money" Maker**. It must be appreciated ... that Paper Money, had certain indelible **Advantages**:

1. To administer the country became much smoother ... also as a **Charge**, as well as an **Act**
2. Tax Collection was Simpler and Less Voluminous; avoiding unnecessary physical exercise
3. All Transport Charges were minimised ... Less Weight and same-ways Less Volume ...
   NO COINS!
4. **Mathematics**: **a.** Polynomial Algebra **b.** Simultaneous Equations (4 un-Knowns) Rectangular Array Coefficients (modern **Matrix**): Elimination by Reduction (1 un-Known) ... Strangely, was invented in 1303: **Pascal Triangle** Diagram. **c.** Spherical Trigonometry: by Cubic Interpolation
   (Astronomical Calculations), for a **Seasons' Calendar**
5. **Medicine**: **a.** Use of **Herbal** Remedies, by Mongol *otachi* Physicians **b.** "Four Great Schools", Chinese Medical Tradition (**Jin** Dynasty heritage): *Acupuncture*, *Moxibustion*, and surprisingly *Pulse Diagnosis*, were currently in use, all over the country ... thus, Total **Modernism**!
6. **Kublai's Mistake** (as Today's West) ... **Don't Make War, Make Commerce in East?**
   in Peace ... & Rest in West?

==='n thus carries on … Tariq Hameed===

Kublai … as an Architect … as a Constructor … and as an Administrator

Kublai repaired a remarkable number of public buildings … and likewise, extended a good number of deteriorating highways. He also contributed to promote the economic growth … such as rejuvenating the existing **Great Canal**. However, the major and most important source of Chinese Revenue being the total monopoly of **Salt Product**, on the National scale, his domestic policy relied on many facets of the age-old Mongol Traditions: thus, some of these methods, in an increased manner did clash, with the established social and economic culture … often frequently. In any case, a compromise was arranged; and Chinese merchants expanded maritime operations, to the South Sea and Indian Ocean.

Chinese Dynasties … 13 Reigns … Thru the Centuries … 2070 BC to 12/02/1912 AD (& 1923-2021)

1	-2070	-1600	**Xia**	Flood Control System	2	-1600	-1050	**Shang**	Maths, Art, Military
3	-1046	-256	**Zhou**	Writing, Coins Confucius	4	-221	-206	**Qin**	Public Works : Terracotta
5	-206	+220	**Han**	Silk Road to Europe	6	220	581	**Six**	Jin & Han : 3 Kingdoms
7	581	618	**Sui**	Literature : Great Canal	8	618	907	**Tang**	Ancient China : Gold Age
9	907	960	**Five**	Dynasties & 10 Kingdoms	10	960	1279	**Song**	Gun-powder, Printing
11	1279	1368	**Yuan**	Mongol Kublai Unites	12	1368	1644	**Ming**	Great Wall Completed
13	1644	1912	**Qing**	Ethnic Manchu: Tributary	…	1912	1949	**State**	**Mao** Communist China

Ser. #	Page	Description
1.	Title	gettyimages-1044825496-612x612.jpg … https://www.gettyimages.fr/detail/illustration/kublai-khan-of-the-mongol-empire-illustration-libre-de-droits/1044825496?adppopup=true
2.	3	**I R I S** … **Eyed** … https://www.publicdomainpictures.net/en/hledej.php?x=25&y=19&hleda=Irises
3.	3	**English** … Beowulf … http://www.pgdp.net … Project Gutenberg … 29 by Samuel Taylor Coleridge
4.	4	https://www.pexels.com/Samuel+Taylor+Coleridge © **Poemine.com** … for educational and informational purposes …Project Gutenberg … 29 by Samuel Taylor Coleridge
5.	6/7	Roma … **Vaticano** … **Italiano** … pexels-photo-6251682.jpeg … https://www.pexels.com/photo/majestic-dome-ceiling-with-fresco-paintings-in-catholic-cathedral-6251682/
6.	6/7	Italia … https://www.pexels.com/photo/bridge-of-sighs-venice-italy-970519/
7.	6/7	**Pakistan** … **Lahore** … **Punjab** … **Islamabad** … https://www.google.fr/search?q=lahore+historical+city&tbm=isch&tbo=u&source=univ&sa=X&ved=0ahUKEwi9gO610bjXAhXMyKQKHc_iAIkQsAQIOA
8.	6/7	**National.Chart.of.Accounts.fr** … My Own Written Chart of A/Cs … on My Own Writ Site http://www.noor-us-samaawat.com/documents/thQ-ChartNc.pdf *thBk-E-01*9-15*.pdf
9.	6/7	**Unicode**.org Consortium … **International Consortium … All Computer Language Codes**
10.	6/7	NADRA Nat. IDs … **Pakistan National Site for ID Cards … Citizens of the World**
11.	6/7	**Microsoft** … **Major International Site, for Computer Softwares … ALL World Citizens**
12.	8++	**Xanadu** … Shangtu … **Khanbaliq** … photo-1483135349295-9e3c48106ee6.jpg … https://unsplash.com/
13.	10/50	That. Spirits .to.the.Ninth.Heaven.Arise …(1923)…https://www.youtube.com/watch?v=nZV2EuA9fwM

Further Reference and Consultation in details … See … **History** : https://www.history.com/topics/china/kublai-khan

… **Ilkhanates** : https://www.ancient.eu/Ilkhanate/   … **Biography** : https://www.britannica.com/biography/Kublai-Khan

… **Mongol Naval Force** : https://www.navytimes.com/news/your-navy/2020/01/07/kublai-khans-mongol-navy/… **You can Click the Links**

6. _Paris_. : _France_. **LA LETTRE À ÉLISE** Romance en Fa (_Beethoven_) F-2-6 (1975)

" **Si fanno Profumi** schiacciando le Rose. ".	" **One makes Perfumes** on crushing Roses. ".
Ora ti racconterò una storia **carina**,	I'll tell you a story **pretty** 'n plain,
pieno di tenerezza e di _Piena_.	full of tenderness 'n _Pain_.
C'era una Volta, lì è cresciuto un giardino.	Once upon a Time, grew a garden here.
Viveva un **fiore** in giardino questo;	'N in this garden Lived a **flower**;
era una Rosa,	'twas a Rose,
la più **carina** di tutte una Rosa **molto** rosa.	prettiest of all a **very** pink Rose.
La rugiada matinale la rendeva più Bella	The morn dew enhanced more 'n more 'tis Beauty
e tutti suoi **Amanti** lì circondavano di Gioia !	'n all 'tis **Lovers** surrounded 'tis with Joy !
A due passi da lei Viveva un'altra Rosa	Just two steps away another Rose Lived
Rosso scuro	Dark red
molto _Arrabbiato_	**well in** _Anger_
dall'ingiustizia ingiustizia di **essere** stato sospeso,	**being** in injustice of slow linger langer,
senza baciare	without a kiss
la sua Cars compagna in Silenzio da adorare.	of his Dear companion in Silent hiss.
Un giorno in mezzo dei due	A day 'tween the midst of the two
sono Passati passi **oscuri**.	Sombre steps Passed t○○.
La Rosa rosa si **inchinò** così„	The pink Rose so **d**own bows„
una **m**ano la prese	then a **h**and it holds
per in una asola a posizionare	'n placed it in the buttonhole folds
in Dolcezza a curare ...	in Soft moulds ...
era ab Belli ta dalla modestia	herself she em Belli shed with modesty
di essere **Amata**	to be **Loved Lovingly**
posseduta ... ♪♪♪ **anche temporaneo** ♪♪♪ ...	possessively ... ♪♪♪ **even temporarily** ♪♪♪ ...
(**Silenzio**) !!! La Rosa **rossa** divien più scura così **Pura**	(**Silence**) !!! The **red** Rose grew darker 'n so **Pure**
si incandescenza	so incandescent 'n more
che dissero tutti i passeggeri	that the passengers said all
" **Com'è** Bello **essere** felici. "	" **To be** happy 'tis how Beautiful. "
Nessuno ha visto la rugiada senza **Lacrime**„	Dew **without** Tears NoOne has ever seen„
ben discordanti scorrono le gocce.	In discord flow drops wherever they have been.
Dopo alcuni giorni	A few days later 'n when
che si asciuga, tutti i suoi **petali** sono caduti„	all dried up, all 'tis **petals** were fallen„
e un'**Ombra tra i passeggeri**	**and among the passengers a** Shade
senza **accorgersene ha** schiacciato **li**.	**crushed** them without **even noticing how**.
Ecco la storia banale la mia piccola _Élise_ !	Here's a banal story my little _Élise_ !
Il giardino **è D**évastato„	**The** garden **is D**évastated„
ma ancora i **Profumi** ci sono	but there still linger **Perfumes**
che si ricordano delle cose Vecchie ...	that remind you of Old causes ...
" **Si fanno Profumi** schiacciando le Rose. "	" **One makes Perfumes** on crushing Roses. "

6. *Paris* : *France*. **LA LETTRE À ÉLISE** Romance en Fa (*Beethoven*) F-2-6 (1975)

♪ " **On fait les Parfums en écrasant les Rosea**. "

♪ Je vais vous raconter une histoire **mignonne**,

♪♪ pleine de Tendresse et de *Paine*.

♪ Aux Temps Jadis existait un jardin.

♪♪♪ Dans ce jardin Vivait une **fleur**;

♪♪♪♪ c'était une Rose,

une Rose **très** rose la plus **jolie** de toutes.

♪ La resée matinale la rendait plus Belle

♪♪ et tous les **Amants** l'entouraient de Joie !

♪ À deux pas d'elle

Vivait une autre Rose

♪♪♪ foncée

rouge

bien en *Colère*

♪♪♪♪ par l'injustice d'**être** figée,

sans embrasser

sa Chère compagne.

♪ Un jour entre les deux

sont passés des pas sombres.

♪♪♪ La Rose **si** rose s'est inclinée,,

♪♪♪♪ une **m**ain l'a prise

et l'a placé en boutonnière

en Douceur …

6.   *Paris.* : *France*.   **LA LETTRE À ÉLISE**   Romance en Fa (*Beethoven*)   F-2-6 (1975)

♪   elle s'est emBellie
par la pudeur

♪♪♪   d'être **Aimée**
d'être possédée ... ♪♪♪ même temporaire ♪♪♪ ...

♪♪♪♪   (Silence) !!! La Rose rouge devînt plus foncée si Pure
si éclatante

♪   et tous les passagers ont dit

♪♪   "   **Que c'est beau d'être heureux.**   "

♪   **Personne n'a vu la** rosée **sans** Larmes„

♪♪♪   Les gouttes coulantes
très discordantes.

♪♪♪♪   Quelques jours après
en se desséchant, tous ses **pétales**
sont tombés„

♪   **et parmi les passagers**
une Ombre

♪♪   **les a écrasé**
sans l'apercevoir.

♪   Voilà ma petite *Élise* une banale histoire !

♪♪♪   **Le** jardin **s'est Dévasté„**

♪♪♪♪   mais il reste encore
des **Parfums**
qui vous rappellent
De Vieilles choses ...

♪   "   **On fait les Parfums en écrasant les Rosea.**   "

... Pour **Nicole** ... **Autodidacte** ...

... **Maître de la Sensibilité de Beethoven** ...

4. Roma : Italia : Italiano   **LE TRE OMBRE**   **La Divina C**omedia (*Danté*) (1989)

Contro il grigio della sera	Against the grey of an eve
tre Ombre	three Shades
si sovrapogono	self super-impose
sul Silenzio del muro	on the Silence of a wall
le Ombre	a Shade
della Vita dispersiva	of a Life dispersed
della Vecchia Signora Disperata !	of an Old Woman Desperated !
" Sono sposato	" Was married
per avere una famiglia	to found a family
e sono rimasto a casa	'n so remained at home
per tutelare questa famiglia;	to up-bring my family;
mi piacerebbe viaggiare,	'twill please me to travel,
mio figlio è già partito	my son's already away
colla sua innAmorata	with his Love
e a lei dispiace	'n it annoys her
quando io mi penso di lui:	when I think too much of him:
mi piacerebbe girare,	'twill please me to go around,
fa molto Freddo questo Autunno	'tis very Cold this Autumn
ma la sola figlia non vuole	but my only daughter wants not
mettere qualcosa addosso	to put any cover on her back
io sento che sarà indisposta	so feel I that she'll be indisposed
poiche il riscaldamento non	as the heating doesn't
funziona encore, che brutta Vita„	function yet, a sorry Life„
nell'Autunno delle nostre Vite:	in the Autumn of our Lives:
mi piacerebbe partire	'twill please me to go away
ma devro fare subito la cena	but must make supper soon
per mio uomo; non ho visto	for my man; havn't seen
i mei Amici per tanto tempo	my Friends since so a long
perchè tutti sono partiti	'cause all are gone
altrove e ora	elsewhere 'n now

4. <u>Roma</u> : <u>Italia</u> : **Italiano**   **LE TRE OMBRE**   La Divina Comedia (*Dante*) (1989)

non ho tanti Amici vicino	remain not many Friends nearby
Nulla Idea da motivo o dove sono,	**N**ull Idea where or whereby,
che brutta **V**ita; il mio secondo	a sorry **L**ife; my second
figlio mi ha chiesto di fare	son asked me to do
una corsa, sono troppo stanca …	some shopping, so tired am I …
ho **dimenticato** la sua domanda	have **forgotten** his needs
non posso farlo e poi adesso	can't do it 'n also now
la **N**onna non sta bene: presto	**G**ranny feels not so well: s**o**-**o**n
devro commenciare la cucina„	must start my c**o**-**o**king„
mi piacerebbe tanto viaggiare	'twill please me much to travel
vedere altre **P**aesi	see other **L**ands
altri **T**empi nel altre **P**aesi	other **T**imes in other **L**ands
ma, no	but, no
come trovare il **T**empo? "	how to find **T**ime? "
E l'**O**mbra della **V**ita **senza V**ita	'N the **S**hades of a **L**ife **L**ifeless
rinforza l'**O**mbra **sfumata**	reinforce a **S**hady **darkness**
della **V**ecchiaia	of **O**ldness
di cosi **V**ecchia **Gran**de **D**onna:	of so **O**ld so of a **L**ady's **High**ness:
" Sono UN SACRIFICIO e sacrificio	" Am A SACRIFICE 'n sacrifice
che non si vede ! "	is when not is seen ! "
E l'**O**mbra della **V**ita	'N a **L**ife in **S**hades
senza far **R**umore	**without** least **N**oise
si **P**erde in **c**repuscolo della **LUCE**	**L**ost itself in the **d**usky **LIGHT**
della **s**era e **c**repuscolo della **LUCE**	of the eve 'n the **d**usky **LIGHT**
della **s**era si ferma qualche ritagli	of the eve faded slight bits
prima di allontanarsi nella **N**ulla„	before disolving off unto **N**ull„
nella **D**ivina **C**omedia **U**mana …	a **D**ivine **C**omedy **H**uman toll …
" Sono per **N**iente ! "	" Am for **N**othing ! "

" Io sono per **Niente** ! Io sono di passagio E ho vuoluto Illuminare Un **Vero** aspetto Vivo della Vita Ma che non è della Vita Può riuscire **Niente** nella Vita. Un fiero **Raggio** in **Conflitto** sto io **Senza** **S**apere **c**he **S**ono **s**tato **Senza c**onsistenza **Senza** utilità, **c**osì **S**ono venuto **solo** ma **solo** **S**marrirmi nei tanti livelli **V**itale che fanno della Vita Una materiale trasparente **R**ifra**g**ente sempre ripresa Dentro il suo **Pri**s**ma** buio **Senza** arrivare a **N**essuna parte Tranne che creare l'**Ombr**e grigie Sovrapposte Che si degradano Contro il muro del **S**ilenzio **I**n**F**ossato Nella **Notte** di **T**empi fungosi … **Nel mezzo del camin …** "	" I am for **Nothing** ! I am only a passage And wanted to Illuminate A **True** aspect Live of Life But who's not of Life Can succeed **Nothing** in Life. A proud **R**ay I've been in **S**trife **Without K**nowing that **W**as **s**ense **Without** consistence **Without** utility, **s**o **W**as coming **alone** 'n **s**ole **W**asting me unto all **s**equels **V**ital which make of Life A transparent material **R**efle**c**ting always to repeat Inside its own **Pri**s**m** darkened **Without** arriving unto **N**owhere **Ex**cept creating **S**hadows greyed Super-imposed Which so degrade Against a wall of **S**ilence **F**ossilised Unto a **Night** of fungy **T**imes **In the mid of the strand …** "

10.   Roma : Italia   **LE TRE OMBRE**   La Divina Comedia (**Danté**)   1989

… **Dante** … https://unsplash.com/s/photos/Heaven and Hell … Unsplash-Hell.Image … Hell …
… Unsplash-Hell.Heaven … Unsplash-Awake and Enter. Heaven-is-here-at your-Door… Heaven …

St. John Climacus described Christian life as a ladder; **demons** *tempt*, while **angels** *encourage* monks. Ladder of Paradise, has thirty rungs. (St Catherine, Mount Sinai)

The Circle of Hell, the Cold Water (1476 Leonardo da Vinci). Codex De Predis, hosted his family in Milan. Cristoforo de Predis, Miniaturist and illuminator.

Spheres Between Heaven and Hell. Neville of Hornby Hours, Luminarium Encyclopedia : **Medieval Cosmology and Worldview**

4. Roma : Italia : **Italiano**   **LE TRE OMBRE**   **La Divina Comedia** (*Danté*) (1989)

La Paura e l'Invisibile	**The Fear 'n the Invisible**
Dante Alighieri … Divina Comedia … *Inferno* !	Dante Alighieri … Divine Comedy … *Hades* !
" Une fôret et son obscurité	" A Forest and its **obscurity**
la peur qu'elle provoque chez l'homme	a Fear which it provokes unto a **man**
et l'apaissement qu'il trouve à sa sortie.	'n the **apaissement** which's found in e**x**it.
Mais des bêtes féroces barrent la route	But such ferocious **beasts** barre the route
dela fuite et du salut sur la colline.	from Escape **'n shelter** on the hillock.
Terreur, reculade et chute de l'homme	*Terror*, reculade **into** slips of **man**
qui se-Noye à-Nouveau dans l'**obscurité** !	who Drowns a New **unto obscurity** !
" Soudain, une ombre sort des **ténèbres**.	" Suddenly, a Shade exits off **darkness**.
C'est une **figure** aux contours **indistincts**	It's a **figure** of contours **indistinct**
car il ne s'agit pas d'un autre homme	as it comes not of an-other **man**
mais d'un revenant.	but of a re-**visitor**.
C'est un Sage, un maître	'Tis a Sage Sage, a Master Master
à la fois puissant et Savant,	Ever 'n always Powerful 'n Wise,
qui va aider l'homme perdu,	Who'll hold a **f**inger of a **man astray**,
guider enfin son initiation	**G**uide 'n re-initiate 'tis **B**eing to be
dans sa quête de la Connaissance ! "	in 'tis ultimate Quest for Knowledge! "
Ce scénique spectaculaire œuvre	This spectacular **sc**enique opens
un poème médiévale très célèbre …	a very celebrated medieval poëm …
(Marcello Castellana)	**(Translation by** Tariq … **Marcello Castellana)**
" **Nel mezzo del camin di nostra vita**	" **At mid of the strand of our life**
mi ritrovai per una selva oscura	me found by a wood obscure
ché la dritta vita era smarrita	that the straight way was lost aduff
Ah quanto a dir qual era è cosa dura	Ah so to say that 'twas a fact so tough
esta selva selvaggia e aspra e forte	this wood so savage 'n sour 'n rough
che nel pensier rinova la paura! " …	that in pensive re-awakes fear enough ! " …
" Per me si va nella Città dolente;	" For me aye go into the City so sore;
Per me si va nell'eterno dolore;	For me aye go into an eternal ache;
Per me si va fra perduta gente; " …	For me aye go 'tween so belost folks; " …
" Della valle d'abisso dolorosa,	" In the vale of an abyss of pain,
Che tuono accoglie d'infiniti guai, " …	Which grants you an infinite strain, " …
(Sulla Porta del Inferno è Scritto)	**(On the Arch-Door of Infernal is Writ)**
" **Lasciate** ogni Sper**an**za, o voi ch'entrate;"	" **Abandon** all Hope, ô Ye who enter here;"
" Ho letto la Divina Comedia in Inglese !	" Have read the Divine Comedy in English !
Un giorno … in Italiano … devo farla !!!	One day … in Italian … must do-it !!!
Tariq HAMEED ! "	Tariq HAMEED ! "

5.   Roma : Italia : **Italiano**   **La Rosa a l'Alba**   Rose-Dew at Dawn   (1993)

Anni fa una Signora italiana mi vide scrivere **qualcosa** e mi chiese cos'era che scrivevo io ? Le ho detto che era solo un'"**Idea**", **qualcosa** di simile alla poesia ma non proprio poesia; che non ho seguito alcuna stabilitata schema, rilasciati **Pensieri** appena: e le "Idea" lente che fluttuano da Sole, iniziano ad avere un Senso„ svelando alcuni Misteri del **Mondo** e della nostra **Vivente Vita**, vengono de-giustificati. Fu così che mi chiese di scrivere **qualcosa** sul'lei„ sul suo nome "Rosalba".

Non scrivo **mai nulla** su ordinazione. Non lo faccio **né** per piacere a **Nessuno né** per guadagni pecuniari. Deve uscire dal cuore. E non faccio **mai** nomi, perché **Nessuno** in questo **Mondo** è **mai** nato con un nome„ gli viene dato solo in seguito, per motivi di **Convenienza**: quindi mi piace rimanere il più **Fedele** possibile alla **Natura**. Fortunatamente, il suo stesso nome era un **tema** poetico; Lascio a voi indovinare di cosa si tratta, che la mia Fantasia si è quasi scatenata e ha volato in giro con un **Ritmo Vibrante** e insistente di "la **Rosa**" e "l'**Alba**" il tutto avvolto da una certa morbidezza, una morbidezza che faceva parte del suo carattere e una certa **Malinconia** perché lei come tutti aveva dei Problemi„ **Problemi Tristi**; e **solo** per citare l'ultimi, il suo Grande **Amore Viveva** a circa quindicimila chilometri di distanza„ ecc. ecc. …

Purtroppo giorni dopo, mi è stata rubata la valigetta e la "pseudo-poesia" non ero capace darle **mai**. Per caso la rividi alcuni giorni più tardi, quando ero molto impegnata in un atto molto "non pseudo-poetico" di vendere due piccoli tappeti; mi ha chiesto sulla sua poesia o che ho provato qualcosa di nuova … Questa volta NON l'ho delusa„ come alcune Idee sono rimaste da prima !!!

A parte i fatti, certe Idee erano ancora appese all'**interno**„ che parte del Iniziale era conficcato nel mio cuore„ ma è stato un compito epico **Ricreare** la Freschezza e la spontaneità dell'originale … ma lasciare la Speranza, **mai**. I **S**entimenti non erano gli stessi„ e **né** lo erano le **Rime** o **Ritmi**; **né** è stato possibile **Ricreare** le inversioni e gli intrecci, de **P**arole con loro giochi subtile„ come multipli di incroci di 'Rosa' e 'Alba' e 'Alba' e 'Rosa', che l'uno divenne costantemente l'altro poi l'uno„ separando e unendo e unendo e separando; un pieno concentrato di **Leggerezza** e morbidezza!

Sì, cì sta il Problema! **Una cosa** Promessa **è pienamente dovuta**. Ma come ripetere un'esperienza di tale **Natura**, senza ispirazioni altrove?

Non chiamando **Nessuno** per nome„ *come destreggiarsi con questi nomi anche di nuovo?*

Avendo fatto ora, una tale promessa, come organizzarla finalmente, "**Per chi suona la campana**?" Ma come i **S**entimenti di questa persona erano sinceri e stabilì, ero incoraggiato! E la LUCE iniziò a **Spunt**are! Così è tornata "La **Rosa**" e tornata "L'**Alba**"! Supponiamo che tu stesso porti il suo nome,, una **Idea** splendida,, cosa potrebbe succedere? E questo successò ... Sono diventato lei,, e i **Pensieri** inizivano a **Spunt**are ... Quindi esce 'Una **Rosa** e un **Alba**',, qualcosa di più tenero, più Profondo,, e più **Umano**. Poi in non più di dieci minuti, giusto il **T**empo di annotarlo su **C**arta, la traduzione. Tale è la **Verità** intera e non diluita,, quindi per favore aiutami,, Il Mio **Ængelo** custode!

P.S.: La traduzione **P**erde parte del suo fascino e della sua Freschezza originali Italiani. Ma la tenerezza ondulata rimane. Anche alcune **I**mma**g**ini possono sembrare state copiate da quanto avevo **s**critto in precedenza,, è solo colpa di aver riutilizzato un po' del materiale **P**erduto,, tuttavia, l'**Idea** di partenza rimane, Fresca come era in origine.

Cosa Quando Dove Qui e Là ... "Il **Mondo** non è Rotondo : ma se è **Vero**" ... Galileo Galilei

---

| 5. | Roma : Italia : **Italiano** | **La Rosa a l'Alba** | **Rose-**Dew **at Dawn** | (1993) |

Years ago an Italian **L**ady saw me **w**riting **so**mething and asked me what was it that **W**riting was I ? I told her that it was only an "Idea", **so**mething like poetry but not **R**eally poetry; that I followed no established schemes, just released **Thoughts**: and "Ideas" Floating slowly on their own, start making **S**ense,, revealing some **M**ys**t**eries of this **World** and of our Lively Life, are de-justified. Thus 'twas, that she asked me to **W**rite **so**mething on her,, on her name "**Rosalba**".

I **n**ever **W**rite anything on order. I do it **n**either to please anybody nor for pecuniary gains. It has to come out from the heart. And I **n**ever mention any names, because **No**body in this **World** was ever born with a name,, it is only given later to him or her, for purposes of **Convenience**: so I like to remain as **True** to **N**ature as possible. Fortunately, her name itself was a poëtic **theme**; I leave it to you to guess what 'twas, that my **F**ant**a**sy sort of self-**un**-leashed and flew around with a Vibe**r**ating and insistant **R**hythm of "la **Rosa**" and "l'**Alba**" all enshrouded in a certain softness, a softness which formed a part of her character and a certain **M**elanchony because she like everyone else had **P**roblems„ **S**ad **P**roblems; and just to mention the least one, her Gr**ea**t **Love** Lived about fifteen thousand kilometers away„ etc. etc. ...

Unfortunately, a few days later my brief-case was stolen and this "pseudo-poem" I could deliver **n**ever. By chance some days back I saw her again, when was very much engaged in an full "un-pseudo–poetic" act of selling two small carpets; she asked me if I had ever found her poem or tried anything a New ... This time I did NOT disappoint her„ as some **Ideas** lingered from afore !!!

Facts despite, that certain **Ideas** still hung **inside**„ 'n parts of the Begins were stuck unto my heart„ but 'twas an epic task to **Recreate** the Freshness and the spontaneity, of the original ... but to **Abandon H**ope, **n**ever. The **S**entiments weren't the same„ 'n **n**either the **R**hymes or the **R**ythms; nor was it possible to **Recreate** the **inversions** 'n the **intertwining**, of the play on **W**ords„ as the multiples of crossings of '**Rosa**' 'n '**Alba**' 'n '**Alba**' 'n '**Rosa**', one becoming constantly the other„ ever separating 'n uniting 'n uniting 'n separating, in a full concentration of **L**ig**h**tness 'n softness!

Aye there Lies the **rub**! **A thing** Promised **is fully due**. But, how to repeat any e**x**perience of such a **Nature**, **without** an Inspiration from elsewhere?

Not using **n**ever any names„ *how to juggle again with these names*?
Having had made now, such a promis„ how to arrange that finally, "**For whom the bell tolls**?" But, the **S**entiments of this person **being** sincere and stable, encouraged me! And **LIGHT** started **Dawn**ing! Thus re-came 'La **Rosa**' 'n re-came 'L'**Alba**'! Supposing, you yourself carried her name„ a spl**e**n**d**id **Idea**„ what could happen? And that did happen ... I became her„ and **thoughts** started **Dawn**ing ... Out came 'Una **Rosa** e un **Alba**'„ **s**o**mething** more tender, more Profound„ and more **Human**. Then in not more than ten minutes, just the **T**ime to jot it **down** on **P**aper, translation included. Such is the whole and undiluted **Truth**„ so please Help me„ My Guardian Ængel!

P.S.: The translation **L**oses some of its original Italian **Cha**r**m** and Freshness. But the undulating tenderness remains. Also a few **I**mag**e**s may seem to have been copied from what I had previously **w**ritten„ it's only the fault of having used a New a bit of the **L**ost material„ none-the-less, the parting **I**dea remains, as Fresh as 'twas originally.

What When Where Here and There ... "The **W**orld is Not Round: but if it's **True**" ... Galileo Galilei

5. Roma : Italia : **Italiano**   **La Rosa a l'Alba**   **Rose-**Dew **at Dawn**   (1993)

La **Rosa** all'**Alba**	The **Rose-**Dew at **Dawn**
non deve **P**iangere	must not **C**ry
perchè dopo tutto,	because after all,
tutta una **Notte**	after a full **Night**
di solitudine	of solitude,
il primo **R**aggio del **S**ole	the first **R**ay of the **S**un
porterá via	will carry away
le sue **L**acrime !	it's **T**ears !
La **Rosa** a **A**lba	The **Rose** of **Dawn**
vi stava una volta	was once
la prima **D**onna	the first **L**ady
in un **G**iardino	in a **G**arden
e salutava con **Joia**	*and greeted with Joy*
il suo cavaliere **errante**	*her* **errant** cavalier
il mag**n**i**f**ico **S**ole	the mag**n**i**f**icient **S**un
danzando	dancing
con **F**ervore	with **F**ervor
un gra**z**io**s**o addio	a gra**c**io**u**s adieu
a la **Notte**	to the **Night**
in tutta la sua **M**ajestia.	in all her **M**ajesty.
E seguì il Valzer **d**ei **P**ianeti	'**N** flowed the Waltz **of P**lanets
Della **Mus**♩**ca** come nei Sonetti	**Of Mus**♩**c** as in Sonnets
Di Giorni oggi **d**opo Giorni passati	**Of** Day in '**n** Day out
Di **Notte d**entro e **Notte** fuori	**Of Night** in '**n Night** out
Di **P**rimavera e**d** E**stat**e e	**Of S**pring '**n** S**umme**r '**n**
D'**A**utunno e d'**I**nverno e	**Of** A**utunn**o '**n of** W**inte**r '**n**
Di **F**reddo e **C**aldo e **D**uro e **M**orbido	**Of C**old '**n H**ot '**n Hard** '**n** M**orbi**d
Di **S**fumature nell'**O**mbre **S**opra **s**otto	**Of Sh**ades hung **Over S**hadows **down**
Di mille **V**erdi nei **P**rati **s**oli	**Of** a thousand **G**reens in **M**eadows **lone**
Di **Colombe** che **A**mano	**Of Doves** which **Love**
Di Nidi **d**'**A**lbero ben in **alto**	**Of** T**ree**-Nests high **above**
Di **S**telle che Luccicano	**Of S**tars which Twinkle
Dei **Cieli** che si **R**aggrinzi**s**cono	**Of** the **Skies** which **W**rinkle
Di Ripetizioni **di In**Si**gnificante**	**Of** Repeats **of In**Si**gnificance**
Della **Fine** che Comincia e	**Of** the **End** which Begins '**n**
Degli Inizi che si **Finisce**!	**Of** the Begins which **End**!

In passato

la Rosa d'Alba

aveva un Amante,

la Profondità della Notte„

e Piangeva perchè

gli Amanti della Notte

pensano che qualche volta

il Vero Amore

si trova nella Profondità

del buio della solitudine:

e più avanza la Notte

più le Lacrime

della rougiada

la rendevano Triste !

Cosi un giorno

la Rosa si è svegliata

e l'Alba l'ha vista

e il suo Signore

il magnifico Sole

si è innAmorato

della Rosa della Notte

e l'ha detto„

" Tu sei il mio primo Amore

e ti do il mio primo Raggio

e ti Regalo l'Alba„

poi ti chiameriò, per sempere,

la Rosa d'Alba„

che mai le Lacrime

della rougiada

ti fanno Piangere

ma vengono solo

per renderti piu bella

e piu Pura. "

In the past

the Rose of the Dawn

had a Lover,

the Profoundness of the Night„

'n Cried because

the Lovers of the Night

think that sometimes

True Love

is found in the Profoundness

of the dark of the solitude:

and more advanced the Night

more the Tears

of dew

made her un-happy !

So was it that one day

the Rose woke up

and Dawn saw her

and her Seigneur

the magnificient Sun

fell in Love

with the Rose of the Night

and said to her„

" You are my first Love

and to you I give my first Ray

and Gift you Dawn„

then I'll call you forever,

the Rose of the Dawn„

that never the Tears

of dew

make you Cry

but to come alone

to make you prettier

and Purer. "

E da questo giorno,	And from that day,
ogni mattina	every morning
la Rosa d'Alba	the Rose at Dawn
salute il suo Amore	greets it's Love
con tenerezza e calore„	with tenderness and warmth„
che tutti gli Amorei	that all the Lovers
del Mondo sognante	of the dreamy World
possono guardare	can see
una Rosa a l'Alba	a Rose at Dawn
con tenerezza e Amore„	with tenderness and Love„
anche quando	even when
nè la Rosa	neither our Rose
nè l'Alba	nor our Dawn
non ci sono più, nè mai !	never are there anywhere anymore !

Rosalba ... a Beauty of a Lady ... married to a person of far away ... often lone ... a request not to be refused ...

Il respiro di un angelo
soffia sulla chiara luna
gonfia il vento
mentre,una leggera brezza
accarezzale tenere fronde
bisbiglia
parole dolci alle nuvole che
teneramente
si commuovonoe lasciano cadere

calde lacrime.
Il sorriso di un angelo
accarezza la timida alba
che rosa
spunta all'orizzonte
e leggiadra
porge la mano al sole.
Buongiorno :-)
(Isabel Allende)

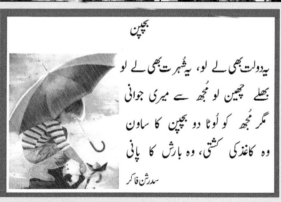

بچپن

یہ دولت بھی لے لو، یہ شہرت بھی لے لو
بھلے چھین لو مُجھ سے میری جوانی
مگر مُجھ کو لُوٹا دو بچپن کا ساون
وہ کاغذ کی کشتی، وہ بارش کا پانی

سدرشن فاکر

Take this Wealth
Take this Fame
Take this Self
Take this Name
But
Render me Back
The Autumn
of Childhood
That Rain-Water
That Paper Boat

11.   Roma : Italia : Italiano   La Rosa a l'Alba   Rose-Dew at Dawn   (1993)
... https://unsplash.com/s/photos/roses and birds ... Rosa ... ed-robertson-UrF1Jf5PamQ-unsplash ...
puck-milder-dj1FWFgIBTg-unsplash ... Text (Poesia) ... (Isabel Allende) ...
... Childhood ... Poetry by Sadarshan Fakir (Pakistan) ... Bird ... Flowers And Birds Pictures ...

8. Marseille **n'a dit à** ... que ... **N A D I A** Naïve, Astute, Doté, Intuitive, Active F-9-8 (1981)

elle n'a dit à l'homme	**que**	:	c'était la **V**ie
	que		c'était l'**amour**
	que		c'était le **D**evoir
	que		c'était **sans** l'**é**sp**oir**
	que	:	c'était *Beau*
il n'a dit à la femme	*que*		c'était trop
	que		c'était la **fin**
	que		c'était **D**estin
	que	:	car et pourquoi **sans** toi
elle n'a dit à l'homme			**sans** moi **sans** soi
			que sera sera
ce	*que*	:	**sans** *être*
il n'a dit à la femme			*peut-être*
			dans un **monde** *d'autres* **être**s
			*l'**être** **sans** Devoir d'**être***
			dans un **monde** *d'autres lettres*
			on peut **être**
			sans **fin** *l'**être** **sans** **fin***
	que	:	l'**é**sp**oir**
elle n'a dit à l'homme			fait **Croire**
	que		la **M**ort n'a pas tort
	que	:	*n'importe*
il n'a dit à la femme			*toi et moi*
	qu'		*on emporte*
	il faut		*sur l'**au-delà***
	que	:	mon **amour**
elle n'a dit à l'homme			tu es **éternité**
	et **que**		**l'infini** **éternité**
	n'est **que**		*même d'après l'**au-delà***

À lire et re-lire de plusieurs façons

(... **essai difficile** par la **multitude** de **sujets** traités ...)

... L'**Histoire** de Vie et **Mort**, **É**sp**oir** et *Désespoir*, **Amour** et **Incarnation** en **Karma** dans l'**Au-delà** ...

puis tout cela s'évolue par la **subtile variation** d'un demi-**M**ot ou de demie-**Pensée**

en quelques peu d'**Images** liées par ces **Rélations** Philosophiques

8.　Marseille　**n'a dit à** ... que ... **N A D I A**　Naïve, Astute, Dear, Intuitive, Active　F-9-8 (1981)

she only said to the man	that	⁚	'twas life
	that		'twas **love**
	that		'twas Duty
	that		'twas **without** hope
he only said to the woman	that	⁚	'twas Beauty
	that		'twas too much
	that		'twas the **end**
	that		'twas Destiny
she only said to the man	that	⁚	'cause 'n why **without** you
			without me **without** you
so			what will be will be
he only said to the woman	that	⁚	**without** being
			perhaps
			in a **world** of other **beings**
			being **without** Rights to be **being**
			in a **world** **w**rit with other lettres
			one **w**ishes to be a **being**
			without end a being **without end**
she only said to the man	that	⁚	hope
			makes **Believe**
	that		Death's not wrong
he only said to the woman	that	⁚	anyway
but must			you 'n me
	that		one continues
she only said to the man			in the beYond
	that	⁚	my **love**
and	that		you are Eternity
only	that		**infinite** Eternity
			even after **beYond**

Can be read and re-read in many manners

(... **a difficult essai** by the **multitude** of **subjects** dealt with ...)

... **History** of Life 'n Death, Hope 'n *Despair*, **Love** 'n **Incarnation** by its **Karma** in the beYond ...

'n so all evolues by many **subtle variations** of semi-**w**ords or only half-Thoughts

in but a few Images linked by these relations philosophic

dans la caVité frappée de Vertige

n'arrête donC pas de tourner

en Cette spirale des lignes conVergentes,

qui trouble la Vision

traumatisant hors de perceptiVe

les Vrais notions des Temps dans la Cage des Âges,

les Idées bêtes de notre Continuité de Chaque jour„

Vous étiez un Enfant Jadis„ C'est Claire !

Où est passé donC votre Corps si Pur si jeune ?

Construit ou Détruit?

Tombé dans un trou VertigineuX de Mémoire ?

En enfanCe

On fait des Choses non-sensées

Comme jouer aveC des bulles de saVon,

Ces partiCules en toutes Couleurs

Des Fées minisCules

Courbant, flottant et se mélangeant„

Soudant d'un ÉClat, la forme des Ar s-en-Ciel

Dans une brève seConde de Beauty Perdu

Pour troubler notre hatiVe Vision„

Mais un soupir les Chassent et elle fuient

Attendant Courts instants

LanÇant la Courts Éternelle

De Desintégration dans les sept bandes d'Ar -en-Ciel rond

Attrapé dans la Coupe d'un Prisme inVisible

Qui ferme Certe son œil

AveC le Coucher du Soleil„

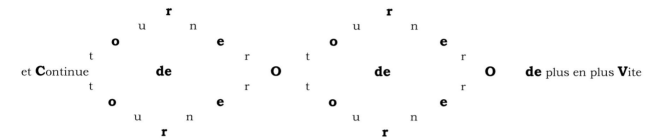

4. Strasbourg **VORTEX** Dans L'**ESPACE** CÉRÉBRALE F-2-4 (1975)

le Temps passe, les Âges défilent, Ces Prismes tournent

```
        r                         r
   u         n               u         n
 o             e           o             e
t               r         t               r
et Continue    de      O        de      O     de plus en plus Vite
t               r         t               r
 o             e           o             e
   u         n               u         n
        r                         r
```

faisant ConVerger Ces lignes spiralées

　　　　　sur Ce point **unique**

　　　　　qui se dilate Courtement

　　　　　dans la **CaVité** Cérébrale

　　　　　le **VorteX** s'approChant,

　　　　　les yeuX se Fermant

　　　　　les oreilles se bouChant

　　　　　auCune **fuite** est permise

　　　　　et le tintement Car aiguë s'amplifie„

　　　　　pour faire **eXploser** dans le CerVeau

　　　　　les Coloris **fantasmagoriques** en abondanCe

　　　　　noir et Illuminé Contre Ce **huis Clos**

　　　　　par un Feu d'ArtifiCe Imaginaire

　　　　　se manifestant en Vérité

　　　　　sur la **Vision** interne en éCran„

　　　　　ainsi Comme un éClair rapide montant

　　　　　au Ciel„ mais **tombe**

　　　　　et ralentit en redesCendant

　　　　　dans Cette sphère fermée flottante

　　　　　des grosses tâChes de Couleurs

　　　　　desCendant,

　　　　　donC de plus en plus lentement

　　　　　pour **s'épandre** dans Cette Sombre atmosphère

　　　　　éClairée insuffisamment

　　　　　d'une Lumière **Cachée** s'étendant„

　　　　　DouCement,

　　　　　Certainement, Sûrement,

　　　　　IrréVocablement,

　　　　　Jusqu'à l'approChe de la faible **ConsCienCe**,

　　　　　Vraiment et Indéniablement **aSSurant**,

　　　　　　　　　Que l'on **retombe** dans l'**inConsCienCe**„

in the caVity struck by Vertige

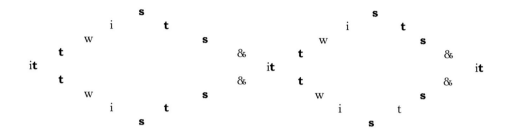

stops thus not to twist

in this spiral of lignes conVergent,
so troubles the Vision
traumatising out of all perceptiVes
that Very True notions of Times just self trap in the Cages of Ages,
into the beastly Ideas of our Continuity of each day,,

Thou *wert an infant of the* Past,, 'tis Clear !
Where went so *thy* Corpse so Pure so *young* ?
Construct or Destruct?
Stuck in a hole VertiginouS of Memory ?

In infanCy

One does things un-Sensed
As playing with bubbles of soap,
These partiCules of all Colours
These Færies minisCule
CurVing, flotting 'n mingling,,
Soldering as Lightening, in Ra nbow forms
Brief a seCond of Beauty Lost
To trouble our hatiVe Vision,,
But a sigh Chases them 'n they esCape
Awaiting Curt instants
LaunChing a struggle Eternal
Disintegrating into the seven Ra nbow bands
Trapped into the Cup of Prisms inVisible
Which Closes Certe 'tis eye

Cast unto the Sun-Set,,

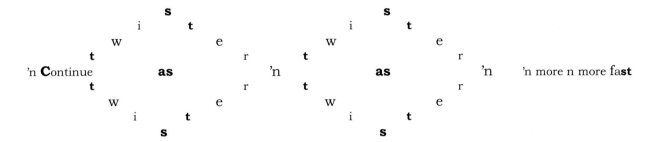

4. Strasbourg   **VORTEX** In The **CEREBRAL SPACE**   F-2-4 (1975)

Time passes, Ages fly by, these Prisms rotate

```
        s                               s
     i      t                        i      t
   w          e                    w          e
  t             r                 t             r
'n Continue        as        'n        as        'n      'n more n more fast
  t             r                 t             r
   w          e                    w          e
     i      t                        i      t
        s                               s
```

to ConVert these spiral lignes

        on so **unique** a point

        which self dilates shortly

        in the Cerebral **CaVity**

        the approChing **VorteX**,

        the eyes self Close

        the ears self buCkle

        no **escape** is permitted

        'n the tintement high pitched self amplifies,,

        to **eXplode** in the Crane

        'n the **fantasmagoric** Colours take abundanCe

        black 'n Illuminated against this **huis Clos**

        by an Imaginary *Fire*-works ArtifiCe

        self manifesting in Truth

        in a **Vision** interne on the sCreen,,

        so as a swift Flash ascending

        to the Sky,, but **falls**

        'n slows down redesCending

        in 'tis sphere Closed **Floating**

        on extended patChes of Colours

        desCending,

        so more 'n more slowly

        to **disolve** in this Sombre atmosphere

        eClaired insufficiently

        by Lights **hidden** extending,,

        Softly,

        Certainly, Surely,

        IrreVocably,

        Until the approaCh of feeble **ConsCienCe**,

        Truly 'n Indeniably **aSSuring**,

                That one **sinks** down into **unConsCiousness**,,

2. *Strasbourg* **Le Poisson** **The FISH** F-1-2 (1974)

↓

↓

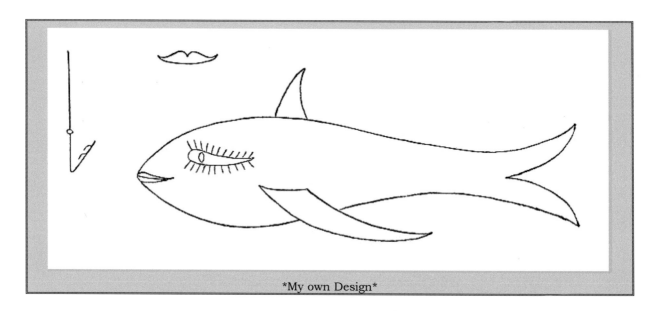

My own Design

Si **Charmant** ce **poisson**	So **Charming** a **fish**
Si **Doux** qui ne sort **jamais** de l'**Eau**,	So **Soft** **n**ever quitting her **Waters**,
Il n'**aime** pas **Déranger** les **Gens**.	No **love** to **Disturb** **Gents**.
Mais des **Gens** viennent	But **Gents** one 'n many come
L'**arracher** de son **royaume** privé	To **snatch** her from her **realms** private
Pour l'emmener dans des **Régions Mortelles**.	To throw her into **Domains Mortal**.
Et il **Souffre** des méchancetés, des injustices :	And she **Sufferers** meanness, 'n injustices :
" Pourquoi ! " se demande-t-il	" Why ! " asks she herself
" Pourquoi moi ? Moi,	" Why me ? Me,
Je n'ai **jamais** fait de *Mal* à personne.	I **n**ever did any *Harm* to anyone.
Pourquoi ?	Why ?
*Peut-être **les lois des Êtres** imposent*	***Perhaps the rules of Beings impose***
*que l'**Innocent** soit puni ! "*	***that Innocents be punished ! "***
Ce **Doux** **poisson** naïf avait bien compris :	So **Soft** a **fish** simple had well **understood** :
La règle de ce Monde est,,	**The rule of this World is,,**
Que la Bêtise doit régner	**That Stupidity must reign**
Et la Beauté n'a pas le droit de Vie !	**And Beauty has no right to Live !**

(Dédié à / Dedicated to ... "Miss" Laforgue) ... et **calme** et **froide** ... so **calm** and so **cold** ...

8. Marseille **Un Papillon se Promène** **Fly - Butter-fly** F-1-2 (1977)

Jamais	**N**ever
un papillon	**a butterfly**
ne vole	**flies**
droit.	**straight.**
Les particules de poussière	Some particles of dust
dans une petite **T**empête de **s**ablière	in a small **T**empest of **s**and
s'étonnaient sur un **papillon**	wondered on a **butterfly**
qui volait en fuyant lentement	who flew flying slowly
de pétale en pétale	from petal to petal
devant tant de pétales.	among so many a petal.
" Tu t'y retrouves? **Pourquoi faire**	" Find you finally yourself? **Why to do**
Autant d'histoires et un trajet si long	**so many stories of so long a pose**
Pour une si Courte **destination !** "	**for a destination so C**lose **!** "
Sa Belle promenade continuant,	It's Beauty promenade continuing,
a rétorqué le **papillon** :	retorted the **butter-fly**ing :
" **La vie si courte É**tant	" **Life so short B**eing
Mieux **autant, que le chemin soit long !**	Better **so, the way lasts so long seeing !**
Je suis la **Joie** d'un jardin	I am the **Joy** of a garden
gracieux„	gracious„
je prendrais le droit sentier	will I take the straight way
desséché quand je deviendrais	when dry will I be away
un tas de poussière	**as a fist of** dust
dans une Tempête **s**ablée	**as a s**and **T**empest Crust
n'ayant ni rève ni Éspoir **!** "	**nor dream nor** Hope **nor must !** "

(Pour **Alexia**, la **Fille de Nadia** à son anniversaire, le 7ième) 1977

     Un papillon a beaucoup de Couleurs . . . . sais-tu pourquoi ???

Il se promène dans le jardin et il prend une Couleur sur chaque fleur qui sourit!

    Il est sage le **papillon** : dans la vie il faut savoir prendre toujours
Une belle Couleur à chaque instant de **bonheur**, ce qui n'arrive pas souvent !

            ma Douceur !

Ainsi je te souhaite des milliers de Couleurs de **bonheur**

        et Beaucoup d'anniversaires pendant longtemps,

            tous plus Beaux, Les Uns que les Autres !

publicdomainpictures.net/en/hledej.php?hleda=butterflies

fantastic-wallpaper-with-butterflie.jpg

pour la **Fille de Nadia**

salut à une femme bien Sage

1977 tu n'avais que **7** ? **2023** ... **56** ?

9. *Alsace* L'**Enfant**, La Mang**OO**ste, Le **Serpent** (Voir la **Bataille**) F-1-9 (1977)

o
∞

|
/\

hypnotisé

d'un *serpent*

l'**enfant**

confiant

innocent

épanoui

par sa **nature**

tends sa **m**ain

pour toucher

jouer avec

cet objet velouté

qui fait si **d**rôle de **B**ruit

sa **l**angue en fourche„

de loin

une mang**OO**ste

voit la s**c**ène

et avec la rapidité

d'un É**c**lai**r**

s'intercale

par son instinct

protecteur

sans **v**olonté e**x**presse

ses **y**eux fixes

bougeant

avec ses **p**ieds

dansant

les **p**as impossibles

la danse

de la Mort„

l'**enfant**

émerveillé

par cette scène

retire sa **m**ain

le *serpent*

peureux

serviteur

de sa **nature**

qui le rend

méfiant

menaçant

prêt à piquer

retient son attaque

ses yeux troublés

T
r
i
n
i
t
é
...

I
n
n
o
c
e
n
c
e

1.

L
a

V
i
e

2.

U
n

P
r
o
t
e
c
t
e
u
r

3.

par ces déplacements

latéraux

très et très rapides

la mang**OO**ste

feint une **indécision**

un bien **L**éger ralenti

le *serpent*

attaque subitement

ainsi une **I**mage

une **I**mage

en deux

qui se découpe

en seizième de seconde

figée en double

ces **I**mages

rendues **immobiles**

par un é**c**lat

de vitesse

se trouve derrière

un coup **sur le cou**

en deux

ou trois

mouvements

imperceptibles

sauf

par une action

lente

vue en rétrospection

au ralenti

termine

la bataille

et puis **disparaît**

prisonnier

de sa **nature**

d'être

le vainqueur

toujours

pour nous **apprendre**

que même

sans **être protégé**

l'innocent

à bien

le **droit**

de Vivre ... ...

o
∞

|
/\

9. Alsace   A **Child**, A Mang**OO**se, A **Serpen**t   (U c a **Battle**)   F-1-9 (1977)

o

oo

|

/\

hypnotised

     by the **e**yes

         of a *serpent*

                 a **child**

         confidant

innocent

         satisfied

                 in his **nature**

         holds his **h**and

     to touch

play with

     this velvety objet

         emitting **funny Noises**

                 his **t**ongue forked„

                         from far

                 a mang**OO**se

         sees the scene

     and with the rapidity

of Lightening

         intervenes

                 by his instinct

protector

     of no e**x**press wish

                 his **e**yes fixed

                       moving

                 with his **f**eet

         dancing

                 in **p**aces impossible

                       the dance

                   of Death„

                 the **child**

         wonderstruck

     by this scene

         retreats his **h**and

     le *serpent*

in fear

     server

         of his nature

              making him

                 diffident

         threatening

ready to sting

         retains his **attack**

              his eyes troubled

Vertical spine text (center column): T r i n i t y ... I n n o c e n c e **1. A L i f e 2. T h e P r o t e c t o r 3.**

---

by his displacements

         lateral

     very 'n very rapid

                     the mang**OO**se

         feigns an **indecision**

     a Light slight slowing

the *serpent*

     attacks suddenly

             as an Image

                 an Image

                     into two

         self-separating

         in a sixteenth of a second

     fixed in double

these Images

         rendered **immobile**

in a flash

     of speed

     comes just behind

attacking his neck

     in two

     or three

     movements

             imperceptible

         ex**c**ept

             in a motion

     so slow

seen in retrospection

as relented

to terminate

         the **battle**

         and then **disappears**

prisoner

of his **nature**

   to be

the conqueror

                     ever

         to us to **teach**

         that even

         on no protection

the innocent

     has well

         the **right**

             to Live ... ...

         o

         oo

         |

         /\

Colour Code Explained　　Spiegazione **Codice Colore**　Code **Couleurs** Expliqué　　Farbcode Erklärt

English	Italiano	Français	Deutsch
Colour Code: TH Invention	Codice Colore: TH Invenzione	Code Couleurs: TH Invention	Farbcode: TH Erfindung
Fast Jump Reading Help	Guida rapida alla lettura	Aide à la lecture rapide	Schnellsprung-Lesehilfe
Eyes self Select Colours	Occhi soli Seleziona Colore	Yeux Choisi les Couleurs	Augen Wählen Farben aus
Grammar: Language **Law**	Grammatica: Legge Languistica	**Grammaire: Loi de Langue**	**Grammatik:** Sprachgesetz
Detectable & Applicable	Rilevabile & Applicabile	Détectable & Applicable	Nachweisbar & Anwendbar
NOR Change **NOR** Diversion	NON Modificare NON Deviare	SANS Modifier SANS Dévier	NEIN Ändern NEIN Umleitung

Fast Reading is an *Eye Jumping Process* : It Allows to **Read Quickly** … by an Intuitive **Text**-Choise by Experience!
La Lettura Veloce è un Processo che Salta degli Occhi : Permette la Lettura Veloce ... Scelta Intuitiva per Esperienza!
Lecture Rapide est un Processus qui fait Sauter les Yeux : Il Permet de Lire Vite … un Choix Intuitive par Expérience!
Schnelles Lesen ist ein Augensprungprozess : Ermöglicht Schnelles Lesen … durch eine Intuitiv Wahl durch Erfahrung!

Grammatical Activity Base is 1. Meaning 2. Anonymes/Synonymes … But NO Concept of **Words Associations!**
Basi dell'Attività Grammaticale 1. Significato 2. Anonimo/Sinonimo … ma con NESSUN Concetto di Parole Associative!
Base d'Activité Grammaticale 1. Signification 2. Anonymes/Synonymes … Mais AUCUN Concept Associative de mots !
Grundlagen der Grammatikarbeit 1. Bedeutung 2. Anonym / Synonym … Aber KEIN Begriff von Wortassoziationen!

These Words Associations have been Analysed by **TH** … Relationships: Spirituality, **Cosmos**, **Nature**, **Human** & … etc!
Queste Associazioni di Parole sono state analizzate da **TH** … Relazioni: Spiritualità, **Cosmo**, **Natura**, **Umano** e Altri ecc!
Ces associations de mots ont été analysées par **TH** … Relations : Spiritualité, **Cosmos**, **Nature**, **Humain** : bien Autres etc.
Diese Wortassoziationen wurden von **TH** analysiert … Beziehungen: Spiritualität, **Kosmos**, **Natur**, **Mensch**, & Andere !

Thus New Groups have been Defined, to Contrast these Classical Omissions, which NO Genious has **Never** ever Tackled!
Così sono stati Definiti Nuovi Gruppi, per Contrastare queste Omissioni Classiche, che NESSUN Genio mai Affrontavò!
Ainsi, Nouveaux Groupes sont définis, pour Contraster ces Omissions Classiques, qu'AUCUN Génie n'a jamais abordées!
Neue Gruppen definiert, um klassische Auslassungen zu kontrastieren, die KEIN Genie jemals in Angriff genommen hat!

Below: Example List of these **Bases** : Devine, Spirit, **Cosmos**, **Universe**; **Nature**, **Human**, Danger, **Nul**, Colours & etc!
Sotto: Esempio: Elenco di queste **Basi** : **Divino**, Spirito, **Cosmo**, **Universo**; **Natura**, **Umano**, Pericolo, **Nullo**, Colori ecc!
Dessous: Exemple: Liste de ces **Bases** : Divin, Esprit, **Cosmos**, **Univers**; **Nature**, **Humain**, Danger, **Nul**, Couleurs etc!
Unten: Beispielliste dieser **Basen** : Göttlich, Geist, **Kosmos**, **Universum**; Natur, **Mensch**, Gefahr, **Null**, Farben: usw.!

- o Devine Divino **Devine** Göttlich ... Devine **Dio** God gods **Love** **A**morato **P**rophet Cupid banjo violini Ideal
- o **Cosmos** Cosmo **Cosmos** Kosmos ... **Cosmo** Galaxy Sky Dawn New Times Watch twinkle tintinnano **inFiniti**
- o **Universe** Universo **Unvers** **Un**lversum ... Universo Universum World Mondo Welt Earth Shore Lake Luna Pluto
- o **Nature** Natura **Nature** Natur ... Spring Summer Autumn Winter Rythms Rose flower rami leaves buds
- o **Animals** Animali **Animaux** Tiere ... **Dog** Cat Locust Crow fly frog croak mole rabbit cuculo snake trout fishy
- o **Aspects** Aspetti **Aspects** Aspektt ... Beauty Sweet dolce Bird færy happy pretty Past Present Futuro Lyes
- o **Contacts** Contatti **Contacts** Kontakte ... Friends **Being** Umana Fanciulla Donna **Mother** O-**Nonno** child Nessuno
- o Water Acqua **Eau** Wasser ... Water Aqua River ripple cloud drop gocce Starts Hazy Horizon Wave
- o Snow/**W**ind Neve/Vento Niegs Luft ... Icicles neve nebbia morbidezza fiocchi Air Cold **H**ot **W**arm **C**aldo **D**ifetti
- o **Mountains** Monti **Montagnes** Bergen ... Mountain Rocce Colline Ground Land Terra Fossa Crevice Granite peaks
- o Forests Foreste Forëts **W**älder ... Trees Legno Valley Meadows Prati Trifogli grass salads Ruscello Stream
- o Colours Colori **Couleurs** Farben ... brown amber pink **red** argent gilt **ebony** green white giallo grey **black**
- o **Shimm**ers Vibra **Chatoyer** **F**limmer ... Ra nbow Lights Images Paint Lustre Hopes Pearls Peace 'n Harmony
- o **My**stery Mistero **My**stére **G**eheinnis ... Know **Purity** **Truth** **Thought** **Pensò** Paradis Fumo sleep LUCE Ombra
- o *Painful* Triste **Douleur** **S**chmerzen ... *Broke* *Pain* *Harm* *Hur* Harsh Conflitto Lacrime Tears **burn** **crush** lonely
- o Sadly Triste **Triste** Traurig ... **Sad** Scream Grief Slave Tragic Silent **Echo** Sound Joke **F**eel tired stanco
- o Danger Pericolo **Danger** Achtung; ... Fear Death Defeat Old AVoid Secret husky *below* Depth whisper Ghost
- o *beYond* Al-delà Al di là Da**Ü**ber ... Above Over **d**own Heaven *Hell* *Fire* Destiny Chance rêve Anima Spirits
- o **Sundry** Vari **Diverse** Verschiedene ... Bound Phantom **End** **Awake** tenebre Visible never **mud** ¶ag♪♫c♪ ♫otes

Urdu … The World Language … Lassan-ul Erd

	Language	Folks	…%...	Family	Branch
1.	Chinese	918	11.922%	Sino-Tibetan	Sinitic
2.	**Urdu**	815	10.584%	Indo-Semetic	Mid-Orient
3.	Spanish	480	05.994%	Indo-Europe	Romance
4.	Arab	466	05.819%	Indo-Semetic	Mid-Orient
5.	English	379	04.732%	Indo-Europe	Germanic

Strange Enough … Most Statistics Consulted … **Ignored Arab** … **Bias**?

In my **Urdu Str**uggle … twice *Threated* was I, by **Elimination**? Why? **Language**? Where it **Hurts**? Only Simple **Language**? …

Questions **Un-A**nswered? & **Un-Wanted**?

1. 1st Slavery Principle: Garbish Speech
2. Talk **Strange** … Eat & Act **Strangers**
3. Ridicule Heritage: do look **Strangers**
4. Till **Nothing's** Left : eXcept **Strangers**
5. **Hon**ourable Nations, are Independent
6. In Action: **Speach** & **Acts** & **Culture** !

… Urdu … Language Distribution … Lassan-ul Erd … Belt & Road …

To **Classify a Language** as a **World Language**, the only Criteria is to estimate … in How many **Worldly** Lands, **is it Spoken**? Thus to take **Chinese**, it is mostly limited in East and South-East Asia … **Spanish**, likewise to West Europe, 2nd. In USA, and mostly in South America … **Arab** has the same case; mostly in the Mid-East and North Africa … **English** is more wide, but is largely rare in South America and parts of North-East Asia … However, **Urdu** is overall the **Banner Bearer**: thus to say **Almost Everywhere**!

Urdu … only to take the Pak-Hind sub-Continent, is astonishing … Pak **205 m**illion; Hind **510 m**illion; Nepal **1 m**illion == **815M**? Here to avoid All Bias & Prejudice, we count NOT the multiple Pak-Hind populations in the 5 Continents … as if 'twas Homeland.

Thus **Urdu** well deserves its **Merited Right** of being called … The Future World Language … Like it or NOT !

Comparing just Statistics, we'll Study … **ISTANS** at **HEART** of the Future Si**lk Belt & Road**.

Pakistan … The Name comes from **P**=Punjab, **A**=Afghan, **K**=Kashmir, **S**=Sind, **tan**=Baluchistan: (Inventor)

Chaudhry Mohammed Ali, in his Book **"Now or Never"** of 28/01/1933: PAKSTAN. *I was added later for H*a*rmony*!

Pakistan has fairly sizable Reserves of **gypsum, limestone, chromite, iron ore, rock salt,** silver**, gold, precious stones, gems, marbles, tiles, copper, sulfur, fire clay and silica sand … now Gas & also Petrol.** Is World Largest **Water Bank**.

Afghanistan … Reserves: **copper,** gold**, oil, natural gas, uranium, bauxite, coal, iron ore,** rare earths, lithium, gypsum, chromium, lead, zinc, gemstones, talc, sulphur, travertine and marble. **Its population is 40 Million,** with a New Regime.

Kyrgistan … Reserves: **hydropower;** gold, locally exploitable coal, natural gas, mercury, nepheline, petroleum, lead and zinc, bismuth, and rare earth metals which are an **important** world **demand**, at present. **Its population is 7 Million.**

Tajikistan … Reserves: **mineral rich country** with more than **600 documented deposits of 50 different minerals;** silver**, gold, lead, zinc, antimony, mercury, molybdenum, tungsten, iron, tin, boron, strontium,** fluorspar, rock salt, precious and semi-precious stones, bituminous coal, anthracite, graphite, mineral wax. **Its population is 10 Million.**

Kazakistan … Reserves: **Oil, coal, various ore and non-metallic deposits** are priceless treasures of the Republic; more famous are chrome iron ore, polymetallic copper, tungsten, molybdenum and uranium ores. **Its population is 19 Million.**

Uzbekistan … Reserves: metallic ores found in (Olmaliq mining belt, Kurama Range); copper, zinc, lead, tungsten, and molybdenum are extracted; there are also substantial reserves of **natural gas, oil, and coal**. **Its population is 34 Million.**

Turkmenistan … Reserves: 200 identified deposits of minerals; **barite; celestine; coal; copper**; clays, such as bentonite and kaolin; gypsum; lead; marble; potash; quartz sand; salt; sand and gravel; sulfur; and zinc. **Its population is 7 Million.**

Azarbaijan … Reserves: **natural gas, iodo-bromide waters, lead, zinc, iron, and copper ores,** nepheline syenites utilized for aluminum, common salt, and Building Materials, marl, limestone, and marble. **Its population is 11 Million.**

Turkey … Reserves: **antimony, coal, chromium, mercury, copper, borate, sulphur, and iron ore**. Nearly half of the workers in Turkey are employed in agriculture, an essential part of the economy. Important crop is cereals, particularly wheat. In 2023, Turkey is being Liberated of its 1st. World War Constraints. **Its population is 82 Million.**

1965 Istanbul, I read Inscriptions in Blue Mosque; old a Turk, *Tears* in **E**yes Embraced me: U can Read it, I can't! 'Tis Crime to Steel History?

Population: Pak=230 M … Afghan=40M … Kyrg=7M … Tagic=10M … Kazak=19M … Uzbek=34M … Turkmen=7M … Azarbai=11 M … Turkey=82 M … So a Faboulous Population of 440 Million: mostly MUSLIM**? Thus a Racial Bias?**

… Urdu is the Main Reason … that the **World** Politics **are** Changing **and a** New **World** is Emerging **… Si**lk Belt & Road **…**

... Urdu ... Language Distribution ... Lassan-ul Erd ... Belt & Road ...

Urdu deserves well, the **Merited Name** ... Future World Language ... 'Tis **Fact** 'n **Reality** !

Comparing **Language** Statistics ... **ISTANS** at **HEART** of the Future Silk Belt & Road.

1. **Afghanistan** Languages: **Dari** is the *Lingua Franca*, in reality Farsi or Persian, about 40% ... Pashto is spoken by 39%, Uzbek 10%, English 3%, Turkmen 3%, Urdu 5%; however Urdu's on rise in recent years: 'n reasonably can be estimated, that because of the New Regime's Interaction with Pakistan ... its Role will become much larger; as per new International needs of the Silk Road arising, a modern **Lingua Comoda**, is the cry of the day.

2. **Kyrgistan** Languages: Till now, **Kyrgyz** was the language spoken mostly at home 'n was rarely used in meetings 'n other events; but, most parliamentary meetings today are conducted in Kyrgyz (simultaneous interpretation). 'Twas written in Arabic script; Latin script was introduced in 1928: subsequently to be replaced to Cyrillic in 1941, by Stalin's orders, resulting from the pending language reform in the neighboring Kazakistan, Kyrgistan in future, will be the only independent Turkish-speaking country, to use the Cyrillic script. Silk Road brings **Urdu**.

3. **Tajikistan** Languages: Tajik 'n Persian languages are very closely related 'n mutually intelligible. The Tajiks' centuries-old economic symbiosis with oasis-dwelling Uzbeks also somewhat confuses the expression of a distinctive Tajik national identity ... Member of the **southwest group of Iranian languages**, is closely related to the mutually intelligible dialects of Farsi 'n Dari in Iran 'n Afghanistan, respectively ... plus **Urdu** in **Pakistan**.

4. **Kazakistan** Languages: 130 ethnic groups live in Kazakistan ... including 65% Kazakhs, 21.8% Russians, 3.0% Uzbeks, 1.8% Ukrainians, 1.4% Uyghurs 'n 1.2% Tatars. Official languages of Kazakistan are Kazakh, with over 5 million speakers (28.57% of the population) around the country, and Russian, spoken by over 6 million people (33.65% of population) ... Now being a Part of the Silk Route, its close links obliges them a **Lingua Comoda**.

5. **Uzbekistan** Languages: One of Turk Languages, belonging to the Karluk branch. Uzbek language is the only official state language, which since 1992 is officially written in Latin script: which was previously the Nastaliq **Urdu** script.

6. **Turkmenistan** Languages: Turkmenistan is the crossroads of World Civilizations; important stop on Silk Road, of main Role in the Muslim World; **a language,** based on Teke dialect is a member of Oghuz branch of *Turkish*.

7. **Azarbaijan** Languages: **Turk Based**, Azerbaijani being a member of Oghuz branch of south-western group; recognized as an official medium in **Dagistan** as well! But, is not official in Northern Iran, where Azerbaijanis exceed. **When one says Turk, one says partly Urdu** ... **'N Noblesse Oblige** ... Silk Road, **Lingua Comoda**.

8. **Turkey** Languages: No language other than Turkish shall be taught as a mother tongue to Turkish citizens at any institutions of training or education - *Art. 42, Constitution of the Republic of Turkey*.
   In **2023**, Turkey is being *Liberated of its 1st. World War Constraints* ... so this a very longly **Dreamt** Middle Corridor, Trans-Caspian China to Europe Connection by railways 'n highways, via Caucasus 'n Central Asia; is viewed as a complement to China's Silk Belt & Road: *an Initiative, but NOT a Competitor.*

9. **Pakistan** ... The Name comes from P=**P**unjab, A=**A**fghan, K=**K**ashmir, S=**S**ind, tan=Baluchi**stan**: (Invented by **Chaudhry Mohammed Ali**, in his Book "**Now or Never**" (28/01/1933): PAKSTAN. **I**, introduced *later*!

   What Miraculous is ... is that the Genghis Army was composed of many Clans & Nationalities; with Languages closely Related to each other: often with similar Sounds or Meanings: eg. *Rehman*'s **Arab**, *Jamhuriat*'s **Turk**, *Kishwar*'s **Persian** ... ALL being an Integral Part of **Urdu** ... so **Urdu** has a **Supra**national **Inter**national *Base*!
   Pakistan Languages: 'n Lastly Not Leastly ... The Miracle Language : **The** Language of the World ... Urdu.
   Originating from the Camp/Palace name of Genghis ... is a **True** World's **Largest** Living **Lingua Comoda**.

1965 Istanbul, I read Inscriptions in Blue Mosque; old a Turk, *Tears* in Eyes Embraced me: U can Read it, I can't! 'Tis Crime to Steel History?

Languages: & Script Changes ... An International Complot & Sabotage ... Alieniate Folks of own History ... **Primary Order Cultural Massacare:** *Faboulous Population? Grand-Millions*: very MUSLIM? **True Racial Bias?**
... **Urdu is the Main Reason** ... that the World Politics are Changing and a New World is Emerging ... Silk Belt & Road ...

... Urdu ... Silk Belt & Road ... History Trace : Past: Present: Future ...

... Past ... The Silk **Route dates from 2nd. BC** ... spanned Asia to the Mediterranean, across China, Himalayas, Arabia, Turkey, Greece, till Italy ... until the 14th. AD: with a heavy trade of Silk, as 'tis name. The secrets of Silk were unknown at that period, which was thus valued in Europe & all southern Russian countries, a major part speaking **Arab**, **Turk** & **Persian**; which then gave rise, after **Genghis'** *Camp or Tent*, to a common Army Language *Urdu*: other items thus traded, included fabrics, spices, grains, hides, works of wood & metal, precious stones & porcelain (of which the fabrication process was likewise unknown)! This important passage had all facilities ... Trading-posts, Markets, Storage, Lodging & Facilities of Commerce. Travelers & traders used Camels & Horses: in modern times, often replaced by Archaeologist & Geographers; of immense impact on **West**: settling even the future **War Ways & Education**, such as gunpowder & paper!

The original Silk **Route dates from the Han Dynasty**. Under **Tang**, 618 to 907 AD. 'twas the Golden Age: serving the development of Science, Technology, Literature, Arts & various Study fields ... instrumental in **Saving Europe from the Dark Ages**: to the extent of spreading Buddhism, Christianity & Islam!

... Decline ... With the advent of newer **Maritime** Routes & the rising Concepts of **Colonialism**, the Silk **Route fell into disuse from the 14th. AC** ... Savage *Commercialisation*, backed by *Industrialisation* lead to an unprecedented period of Catch & Capture: lasting about 5 centuries; until the Death Blow came to **Direct Colonialism**, in the shape of Communism, Nazism and a **Feeble** sort of Fake Humanitarianism, surprisingly? Thus a 1st. & 2nd. **World War** ... with the Liberation of **Pakistan**, India & eventually **China**!

... Present ... The Awakening of the Silk **Route dates from 2013** ... China which considers the 19th. Century as the **"Century of Humiliation"**, due to the **Opium Wars** & the entire population being reduced to a **Nation of Opium-Sleepers**, Woke-up by a Peasant's Revolt lasting 30 years ... Re-organised to start looking at the World in the Face: thus enabling an **Elevation** of the **Poor-Classes** to an Honourable Life!

Nothing is yet certain ... because POWER **can PLAY strange PRANKS on the** POWER-HOLDERS ??????? However, **China** since thousands of years has NO History of Colonialisation ... so 'tis hoped that errors such will NOT be enacted and that ... **Humiliation Hounded in Honour, Homes Humility and Humanity** ??? Thus is the Story of the renewed Future Silk Belt & Road: a **Hope for Equals to be Equals in Honour!**

... Gawadar ... The **South-most** Land-**Port** of the Silk Belt & Road ... One of Major **Deep-Sea** Ports, which can harbour over 500 Large Ships, at a time. It belonged to the Khan of Kalat, who hosted an **Oman** Prince & then gifted it to him in 1781. Negotiating, Malik Feroz Khan Noon, re-obtained it on 8th. Sept. **1958**!

... Future ... The ISTANS at HEART of the Future Silk Belt & Road ... Over 60 Major Countries will benefit; but the massive Land-Block remains ever Pakistan, Afghanistan, Kyrgistan, Tajikistan, Kazakistan, Uzbekistan, Turkmenistan, Azarbaijan, Turkey ... Each Language having Words in **Urdu**: a **Lingua Comoda**.

1. Direct Multi Gold Standard: ... Inter-Country Exchange Values, or through Gold equivalent: *Thus* **$$ Buried**
2. Monopoly **Mineral** Resources: ... All Rare Metals, Minerals, Raw-Materials, Precious Stones & You name it
3. **Solar** Clean Energy: ... Pollution Pure, Ecological, Non-Emission, Electrical & Recyclable Cars & Vehicles
4. **Water** Dominance: ... Mountains, Glaciers, Lakes & Rivers, constitute enormous Reservoirs of Soft Waters
5. Woods, **Trees** & Plantations: ... Forests & Natural Safe Havens abound, protecting precious **Flora & Fauna**
6. Access to **Warm** Water Oceans: ... All Asia, with over 20 Lands: finally finds an easy Way to Warm Waters
7. Space **Research**, based on **Multi-G**: ... To be commonly shared & equitably distributed, for Global **Welfare**

& Pakistan's Language: 'n Last Not Least **... The** Miracle **Language : The** Language of the World **... Urdu.**

Urdu deserves well, 'tis **World Merited Name ... Lassan-ul-Erd ...** 'Tis **Fact** 'n **Reality** !

... Urdu ... Traditional Silk Route ... History : Trade: Culture: Peace ...

... Origin ... Dubbed Silk **Route**, as heavy Silk trading that took place since 2nd. BC; initial monopoly being of **China** on this valuable product: but later the secret spread. Simultaneously, the route facilitated also trade of other goods; fabrics, spices, grains, fruits & vegetables, hides, wood & metal works, specially precious stones & porcelain ... spanning Asia to the Mediterranean: Himalayas, Arabia, Turkey, Greece, till Italy (Venice)! The Silk route included Groups of Trading Posts & Markets, to help in Storage, Transport, Lodging & Commerce Facilities, and other goods Exchange: used were Camels & Horses, as light and fast. Modern Archaeologist & Geographers, follow suite! This led to a common basic **Language** *Urdu*, for a major part of **Arab**, **Turk** & **Persian** speakers; based on the name of **Genghis'** *Camp or Tent*! (**Language** of Peace)! **But Strangely**? Gunpowder & Paper settled the future of the **West's War Monger Ways & Education???**

The original Silk **Route dates from the Han Dynasty**. Under **Tang**, 618 to 907 AD. 'twas the Golden Age: serving the development of Science, Technology, Literature, Arts & various Study fields ... instrumental in **Saving Europe from the Dark Ages**: to the extent of spreading Buddhism, Christianity & Islam!

... Span ... Let's now Study, the **Ancient European Civilisation** ... Antiquity Polygon ...

1. **Pharaonic**: Egyptian, before **3100 BC** (United/Divided); until the country fell to Greece in 332 BC.
2. **Hellenistic**: **Classic Greece is West cradle**; Political **Archetypes** & Ideas, Philosophy, Science, & Art. They had NO Religion: but Myths, explaining Nature ... **Mingling God** & **Man** (**Jupiter's Roman Belief**)
3. **Roman**: **Total Greek Base**! From Julius Caesar Empire ... **Augustus**, golden age of prosperity; the 'Tis fall in 5 A.D. was the most **dramatic implosion** in the human civilization history.
4. **Dark Ages**: **500 years**! After Classical Antiquity, ensued a Surprising Epoch, NO Explanation; when Knowledge, Libraries & All Reason was Destroyed, named "**Dark Ages**" by Petrarch. Light Versus **Ignorance** (Paucity of Written Records, 5-9 AD): State devastated by Visigoths & **Vandals** (**Vandalism**)!
5. **Orthodox Church**: **Evolution**! Roman West Chuch declared forfeit, after the Stunned Defeat of a 3rd. Crusade by Salahuddin Ayubi (**Saladin**). Later all Crusades Failed, including the 8th. The Eastern Church was established at Constantinople, defeated by Sultan Fateh, by Passing Ships over Hills, to storm the Bosphorus ... Then the **Orthodox Church** took over! It was basically Russia, who was the cause of Turk Containment; the Crushing defeat of the Ottomans in **1699** AD ... **January 26**: **Treaty of Karlowitz** (Turkey & Venice, Poland, Austria) ... *Turks quit C-Europe* ... Role of Turks in Europe Ends!

... Colonialism ... Maritime Incursions ... The Shortest Lived Empire, in the History of the World: **300 years**! **2 Centuries of Humiliation**! It Started with **Aggression** on **E**ast ... **A**frica, **I**ndia, **A**sia (with **China**) ... It can be Divided into 3 Elements: **1.** Water Warfare **2.** Industrialisation **3. 2 World Wars**. However, with the Atom-Bomb Blast of Hiroshima & Nagasaki, West Signed its Death-Warrant for ever! Immediate, Liberation of Colonies ... Thus in a 100 years, **the Sun will Set on the Western Front** ... **East** was Humbled, but has **NO Claims** on Revenge ... Remember: Sun, Prophets & Peace, **Rise Ever in East**!

... Modern Colonialism ... Camouflage Wars ... The 2nd, World War ended, but was devised the **Hidden Rule** ... Simple & Efficient ... Based on Power-Holders (West) **1.** Corrupt Officials **2.** Bank Accounts at Power-Holders **3.** Money Laundering **4.** Off-Shore Holdings **5.** Amnesty Granted (Lipwise).

... Hidden 9th. Crusade ... Reality ? ... **Human Beings** Cannot Change their Genes! However, NEW WORLD, with the Population we have, MUST COME TO TERMS! Choose Peace or the **END**!

China: NO History of Colonialisation! **Humiliation Hounded, in Hon urable Homes Humility & Humanity ???** Thus is the Story of the renewed Future Silk Belt & Road: a **Hope for Equals to be Equals in Hon ur!**

... Future ... ISTANS at HEART of the Future Silk Belt & Road ... & Urdu: a Lingua Comoda.

... Urdu ... Future Silk Belt & Road ... 'Twill be : Peace: Technology ...

... North of Equator ...
The known World was Limited to **East** of **Atalantic** & **West** of **Pacific** ... The Cape of **Good-Hope**, was discovered by Vasco de Gama, when using the Triangular Sails againt Wind (Arab Invention) established the **1st. Euro Colony** in India (1510)... Thus till the 16th. AD, the **Active** World was **North-Afro-Eurasia**: the **rest** being the **Unknown Continents**; **A**mericas, **A**ustralias, **A**ntartic (+ **A**rctic). When Galileo affirmed, that World was Round, he was put on the Gallows (1615), his Historic Italian Phrase, "Il Mondo non è rotondo", adding "ma é Vero" **"Tis True"**, saves his Life: making a **fO-Ol** of the set **Church**! Churches, Missionaries, & **Mullah**ism: only Solve a **Mystery** by another **Mystery**: so **Blind Lead Blinds**! Apart from this Land-Mass, there existed another **Tri-Division** on the Water-Front ... The Active Oceans!

... Cold Sea ...
South of Arctic & scans an entire Siberian Land-Span, is Snow-Bound, most year ... Thus Communication is scarce & like-wise Trade; leading most East Euro-Asia to seek **Partners of W**armth!

... Mid Sea ...
Binding **North Africa, West Europe, West Asia** ... known **Cradle** of known Civilisation! This lead to Unprecedented **Maritime** Expansion, as Sea-Span was Limited, Storm-Conditions were Limited, Distances were Limited, Neighbours Near; giving Free-Chance to Fight at Home & Dominate Gents of Peace!

... Warm Sea ...
The Indian Ocean, which gives Birth to the Gulf-Stream; warming West Atlantic & circling round the Brit-Iles, thus Moderating the Channel & **West Europe** ... **NO Gulf-Stream, NO Europe**! Today, the Entire **World** is Searching **W**arm-Waters for Peace: Trade in Peace: in Short ... to Live in Peace! West has **NO** Other **C**hoise but to **Change** Politics, Hippocracy, Attitudes: **Equals so be Equals in Ho**nour! **N**othing is yet certain ... for POWER-Holders **can PLAY strange PRANKS on** POWER-HOLDERS ???????

... Future Polygon ...
How'll All shape-out? **Foreseen Interaction** is **Undefined** ... **Probabilities**?

1. **China**: From a **Nation of Opium-Sleepers**, Woke Peasant's Revolt of 30 years ... Re-organised to start looking at the World in the Face: thus enabes an **Elevation** of the **Poor-Classes** to an Honourable Life! **History Proves** ... thus being Self-Contained over 6000 years, it'll maintain its Non-Expansion in Peace!
2. **Russia**: **Vast Span & Scarce Habitants**; Needs Warm-Water Outlets: only by Teaming-up with its Old Soviet Partners (Ukraine, Byelorussa, Armenia, Georgia) **Enmities** lead **Nowhere**. (Peace **with China**)
3. **Arabs**: **Once Rose from a Small Town, Madina,,** to Conquer Empires ... **Let Asleep Giants Lie** ... Once Awoke, Conquered Millions of Km/Sq in 10 yrs; includes Holy Lands: **Nobly & H**olyly!
4. **Persia**: **Inspired by Persepolis (515 BC)**! 'Tis Culture filters India! Most long Extensive Borders today are Afghanistan (North), Pakistan (East); Links Undeliable. **Geo-Dicts** Destiny : Live Together in Peace!
5. **Istan Areas**: **Mainly** Muslims**; so Common Interest will Unite**! West: **Superior Race** Concept **Fails**.

... Indian Role ...
Balkanisation on way ... West Wants **China War: a planned Broke-up** Pakistan! Mission Impossible, as 'Tis the shortest way to **W**arm-Waters, where an Infra-Structure exists! 'Tis Future!

... Belt & Road ...
Belt is Land-Bound & comes from the Unending Himalaya Mounts **Belt** Ranges ... **Road** is **Sea**-Bound & comes from the Unending Maritime Ship-Corridors, named in Past, as a **Sea-Road**!

... Real Future...
White West **Technological Industry is totally** China Based: Cheaper Fabrication! **Enormous Research** has put China, on the **Fore-front** of Scientific Impossiblities: **Modernism Cumulation**!

1. **6G Broad-Band Data-Networks**: **V**irtual & **H**eterogenic **A**ugmented **R**eality (**VR/AR**); in **Terahertz**!
2. **S**pace & **S**pectrum: to Save our Green & **Blue Planet**, Recyclable **S**pace Technology's an Essential! Clean Ecological **Earth**, Clean-Eco **Solar** Energy, Clean-Eco **S**pace & **Cosmos**, & Clean-Eco **Humanity**!
3. **Nota**: 'Tis Time **Dawns** to Wild White West, a 1/4th. Rest of **Humanity** is **non-Expand** Peace-Loving!

Urdu deserves well, 'tis World **Merited Name** ... **Lassan-ul-Erd** ... **'Tis Fact 'n Reality** !

Tariq Hameed ... **Personal & Family History**   (Deutschland Hannover 1993 Onwards)

Healing with verse ... Book of My Niece ... Zahra

Homage to my Dear Niece : Daughter of Kausar Hameed (Kochi-ji) ... A **True Image of my Mother**

Zahra Hameed debuts an Anthology of Poetry ... Intimate Thoughts on Mental Health, Love & Relationships

Mental Health, no more is a Taboo: What in Past was Troublesome, is simply looked on now as a Brave 'n Courageous, that one Talks over it!

Burning Champa

Deciduous tree is an Apocynaceae: of Cultural Belief in most of Orient.

In a Similar Vein, Several of the DewaneZahra's Poëms in her Anthology allude to the Trepiditions and Joys of a Relationship 'tween a Man and a Woman. Zahra, it is possible, may even talk about herself ... but the Emotions are Universal!

What does a Man do ...

To make a Woman feel Loved?

A Man Notices Tiniest Things,

Like Un-fallen Tear in my Eye!

https://uns plash .com/ s/pho tos/pl umer ia-rubra

Plumeria Rubra ... photo-1619516794122-c189bb741a5f.jpg ... photo-1619516947016-06223e8d61c8.jpg ... photo-1599351334993-b7a1c6cd774f.jpg

Urdu Translation of some Sufiana Verses ... (2021)

My Brother at the Great Wall of China ... (2008)

Zahra's Quatrain : **to whisper stories**

کہانیوں کی سُنسُنابٹ   کِرن ڈھرن کی سُرسُرابٹ
پرچھائیوں کی خرگت   ذریعہ مینہ ٹِبک ٹِبک میں
آتِش جلن کی ڈھک ڈھک   گھر تُمہارے آندر میں
گمشدہ گُمشدہ تھکّن تھک   تند نمرے مَندَر میں !

07:37 ✓✓

To Whisper Stories
Of What We are going to do
Our Silouhettes move in Rainy Windows
So Burn I Slow 'n Fast ... so, so Lost ... Inside of You.

... Now Rendered to an Expanding **R**hymed Quatrain ...

100. Troyes   **Family Tree** ... Hameed & Cie. ... (8 Generations Lahore)   Reality-8- **2019** -99--293-

G-**G**-**G**-**G**-**G**-Grand	7	Hafiz Allah Baksh	**Qura'an**	Memorised
G-**G**-**G**-**G**-Grand	6	Hafiz Hidayat Baksh	**Qura'an**	Memorised
G-**G**-**G**-Grand	5	Hafiz Qadir Baksh	**Qura'an**	Memorised
G-**G**-Grand	4	Hakeem Kareem Baksh	**Hakeem**	Medicine
Great-Grand	3	Hakeem Shams Deen	**Hakeem**	Medicine
Grand-Father	2	Mian Siraj Deen	(Supdt. Of a Directorate)	
Father	1	**Khan Sahib** Mian Abdul Hameed (**BA LLB**)	(LSMF) Dr. Begum Meraj Hameed **Suharwardi**	
Tariq (MA Eng. : ACA, Lon. : IT, Fr)		**Kausar** Hameed (MBA)	**Tahira** Hameed (MSc)	

(Hand written by Nazir Ahmed Jia'baji) ... DG Lahore Municipal Corporation

Daughter Shaheena Married Shahnawaz Zaidi (Chairman Fine Arts : Lahore University)

Nazir A.J. was married to Mumtaz Apa ... Daughter of **M**aulvi **M**ohammad **A**zeem (My Ustad)

In the Musafir Qabaristan (Garhi Shahoo) we have many graves ... of the **two** parts of our Family

1.   **Father** ... Syed Abdul Hameed : Mian Abdul Hameed : Mumtaz Apa : Begum Meraj Hameed

2.   **Mother** ... About 20 of the **Suharwardi** (Khwaja) Family, including 5 of our maternal Uncles

---

The name of our Nana (Maternal Grand-Father) was Ghulam Mohammad ... Nani (Maternal Grand-Mother)

was Ayesha Bibi or Begum ... per the Medical Degree of Khala Jan, found by younger son.

She passed in the year 1934 and Parveen Apa was born in 1931 ---all verified---

Sisters ... Sardar : <u>Mumtaz</u> (<u>Married</u> **S**. **A**. **H**ameed) : <u>Saeeda</u> (2nd of **S.A.H.**) : Meraj

Sardar Married **M**aulvi **M**ohammad **A**zccm (My Ustad) ... Had Naseem; Parveen; Naeem.

Maulvi **M**uhammad **A**zeem (My Ustad) ... Married 4 Times (Never 2 together) Sardar was 4th.

Syed Abdul Hameed ... Married twice ... Mumtaz died (Sutan; Kishwar) ... then Saeeda (Nasreen)

Our **Maternal** Grand Father, **Ghulam Mohamad**, was the first Muslim Magistrate in Kashmir ... **Poisoned**

Ayesha Bibi or Begum was left a Widow, with 4 girls ... their only brother died at an early age.

Sardar & Meraj became Doctors : **L**udhiana **S**tate **M**edical **F**aculty ---*Early Batches*---

The Brother of Nana, Sagheer **Suharwardi**, then looked after the entire Family.

Meraj became the Superintendent of Bostel Jail Lahore ... for Political Grand Dames.

She knew all Grand Ladies of India thus ... to the extent of playing cards with Indra Ghandi.

Indra, as Prime Minister, invited her to India on an Official Visit: being now a Widow, she could not go.

CPs. 10 & 18/11   65   65

یہ مختصر تحریر ایک اعتبار سے غیر معمولی بھی ہو جائے گی ۔ اس عدالت سے صادر ہونے والے فیصلے انگریزی زبان میں تحریر ہو رہے ہیں ۔ انگریزی زبان عام فہم نہیں ہے ۔

مقدمات کی کارروائی کے دوران، عدالتوں کے اندر بسا اوقات یہ تاثر ملتا ہے کہ اکثر دکلاء اور بعض جج صاحبان بھی اس زبان پر اتنا عبور نہیں رکھتے، جتنا درکار ہے ۔ نظام عدل کسی بھی زبان پر جتنے عبور کا تقاضا کرتا ہے ، اتنا عبور انہیں حاصل نہیں ہے ۔ اس مسئلے کی جڑیں ماضی میں دور تک تلاش کی جا سکتی ہیں ۔ جب دکلاء اور ججوں میں عدالتوں میں زیر استعمال زبان کے کماحقہ فہم کی ہے تو عوام الناس کا کیا حال ہوگا جن کی اکثریت انگریزی سے واقفیت نہیں رکھتی ۔ ایسے میں ذرائع ابلاغ میں عدالتی فیصلوں کی درست تفہیم مشکل ہو جاتی ہے اور بحث و تجزیہ کے دوران گفتگو اور سوچ ، واقعات اور حقائق سے ہٹ جاتی ہے ۔

عوام الناس محض یہ تجزیہ نگاروں اور قانونی "پنڈتوں" اور "ماہرین" کے محتاج ہو کر رہ جاتے ہیں ۔ یہ صورت حال بعض اطمینان بخش نہیں ہے ۔

پاکستانی عوام کی اکثریت کو اپنے آئین اور آئینی حقوق کے بارے میں آگاہی کے لیے دوسروں کا سہارا لینا پڑتا ہے اور انہیں مختلف تجزیہ کاروں کی تشریحات اور تاویلوں کی جانچ پڑتال یا تنقید کا خود اس وجہ سے موقع نہیں ملتا کہ عدالتی فیصلوں کی زبان ان کی سمجھ سے باہر ہے ۔

جہاں مندرجہ بالا تقاضوں کی اہمیت ہے ، وہاں آئینی تقاضوں پر نظر ڈالنے کی بھی اشد ضرورت ہے ۔

پاکستان کے آئین میں "بنیادی حقوق" کا باب بے حد اہم ہے ۔ اس کے آرٹیکل 28 میں کہا گیا ہے کہ "مختلف زبان، رسم الخط اور ثقافت کا حامل شہریوں کا کوئی بھی حصہ یہ حق رکھتا ہے کہ وہ ان کی حفاظت اور ترویج کرے اور آئینی تقاضوں کو مدنظر رکھتے ہوئے اس مقصد کے لیے ادارے قائم کرے ۔" اس کے علاوہ آرٹیکل 251 (1) میں یہ واضح طور پر کہا گیا ہے کہ پاکستان کی قومی زبان اردو ہے ، مزید یہ کہ نفاذ آئین کے پندرہ سال کے عرصے میں وہ تمام ضروری اقدامات و انتظامات کر لیے جائیں گے جن سے اردو زبان سرکاری اور دیگر مقاصد کے لیے رائج ہو جائے ۔ اب تک اس آئینی تقاضے کو پورا کرنے کے لیے کسی جامع اور ٹھوس منصوبہ بندی کے تحت کوئی خاطر خواہ قدم نہیں اٹھایا گیا ۔ گو آئین کے نفاذ کے 37 سال سے زیادہ عرصہ گزر چکا ہے ۔ یہ پوری قوم کے لیے لمحہ فکریہ ہے ۔

اس فیصلے کا ایک مقصد یہ بھی ہے کہ آئین کے آرٹیکل 28 اور (1) 251 کی پاس داری 66

کے لیے ایک قدم بڑھایا جائے لیکن اس سے بھی بڑھ کر مقصود یہ ہے کہ آئینی فیصلے براہ راست عوام تک پہنچانے کی کوشش کی جائے ۔

یہاں یہ کہنا مناسب ہوگا کہ قانونی فیصلوں میں انگریزی زبان کا استعمال فوری طور پر ترک کرنے کی نہ تو ضرورت ہے اور نہ ہی اس فیصلے کو اس کی سفارش سمجھا جائے ۔ تحریر تفصیلی انگریزی فیصلے کے اہم نکات کا اردو پیرایہ ہے تاکہ عوام براہ راست اس سے استفادہ کر سکیں ۔

(دستخط : محمد جواد خواجہ)   Jawad Khwaja   CPs. 10 & 18/11

(Short Order)   4-3-2011

[175A(2)]

[175A(9),(10)]   2010   175A   19   2010

18

Chief Justice of the Pakistan Supreme Court for only 24 days …

The Honourable Justice Jawad S. Khwaja: a Gem!

When I had made too-oooo much Noise on Urdu All-Over, he sent me a massage by a Dear Reporter Friend that my Life was in Danger … so was advised to just SHUT-UP my Big Mouth! And that the Supreme Court on its own will Take due Action at Appropriate Time come …

On the Last day of his tenure, Done was Done! Parliament & Cabinet Team & Qaumi Zuban were Instructed to Report on the Installation of the Official PAK Language: but on their Dilly-Dallying, after his tenure the Traitors & BurocRATS proved that the RATS remain always RATS! But Struggle Ever Continues! Tariq_Hameed

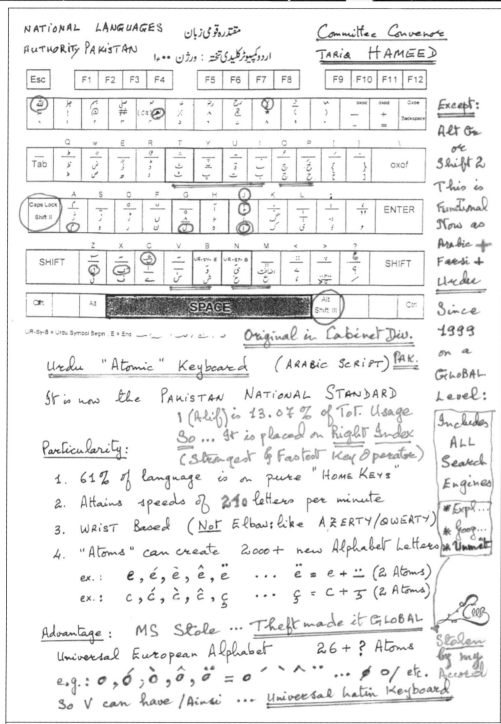

NATIONAL LANGUAGES AUTHORITY PAKISTAN

مقتدرہ قومی زبان

اردو کمپیوٹر کلیدی تختہ : ورژن : ۱۰۰۰

Committee Convenor
TARIQ HAMEED

Except:
Alt Or
or
Shift 2
This is
Functional
Now as
Arabic +
Farsi +
Urdu
Since
1999
on a
GLOBAL
Level:

Includes
ALL
Search
Engines
* Expl…
* Goog…
* Unmet

UR-Sy-B = Urdu Symbol Begin : E = End

Original in Cabinet Div.

Urdu "Atomic" Keyboard (ARABIC SCRIPT) PAK.

It is now the PAKISTAN NATIONAL STANDARD

I (Alif) is 13.07 % of Tot. Usage
So … It is placed on Right Index
(Strongest & Fastest Key Operator)

Particularity:

1. 61% of language is on pure "HOME KEYS"
2. Attains speeds of **210** letters per minute
3. WRIST Based (Not Elbow: like AZERTY/QWERTY)
4. "Atoms" can create 2000+ new Alphabet Letters

ex.: e, é, è, ê, ë … ë = e + ·· (2 Atoms)
ex.: c, ć, c̀, ĉ, ç … ç = C + ح (2 Atoms)

Advantage: MS Stole … Theft made it GLOBAL

Universal European Alphabet   26 + ? Atoms
e.g.: o, ó, ò, ô, ö = o ´ ` ^ ·· … ø o/ etc.
So V can have /Ainsi … Universal Latin Keyboard

Stolen
by my
Accord

ELECTRONIC DICTIONARY
of Localization of Computer Applications
[English-Urdu]

Center of Excellence
for Urdu Informatics

NATIONAL LANGUAGE AUTHORITY ISLAMABAD
(PAKISTAN)

Urdu Tariq Computer
Microsoft Sponsored

This is the Story of my Life : in 3-D Colours … as "Muqamaat"

Like a Qirat High-Lighted in 3-D Space … by the "Vibrating Variations" of Voice

.1. **Letter-Shape Grouped**

.2. **61% Letters on Home**

.3. **Wrist + Finger NO Arm**

.4. **New Lets: New Scripts**

.5. **Military Codes Ability**

.6. Line.1 30: **2.** 61 **3.** 9%

.7. For **Universal** Usages!

Microsoft

مقتدرہ قومی زبان، پاکستان
National Language Authority
Govt. of Pakistan, Cabinet Division

Microsoft Office and Windows XP
Microsoft Urdu Localization Project 2004-05 (1 Year)

۱۳–اپریل ۲۰۰۱ء
اُردو سافٹ ویر مقابلہ
جناب طارق حمید
کی خدمات کے اعتراف میں
نشانِ مقتدرہ

Memo of Participation

*Certified that that Mr.*_____ Tariq Hameed

_____ جناب طارق حمید

has been associated with the Project as

(Technical Validater) ٹیکنیکل ویلیڈیٹر

He performed his duties with full passions and hardworking. He has carried out his duties diligently qualifying the standards of Microsoft tasks and needs of Urdu assigned to him were found magnificent.

پروفیسر فتح محمد ملک
Prof. Fateh Muhammad Malik
Chairman

ڈاکٹر عطش درانی
Dr. Attash Durrani
Head Urdu Informatics

طارق حمید

Urdu Seminar
06/06/1999

24 - 26 MARCH 2001

1st. Software Urdu
Pak Competition
Tariq Hameed
Was the TRUE
Heart & Soul

NATIONAL LANGUAGE AUTHORITY PAKISTAN
FULL MEMBER OF UNICODE INC.

اُردو سافٹ ویئر کا اوّلین مقابلہ و نمائش

FIRST URDU SOFTWARE COMPETITION & EXHIBITION

Urdu **Computer in 30 seconds**: 1. Windows 2. Parameters 3. Date & Language 4. Add 5. Apply & 6. End

Atomic Alphabet: Letters, Dots, Accents (Top/Low) Atomised ... (UniCode 'Diacritics') ... 7 Concat-Images.

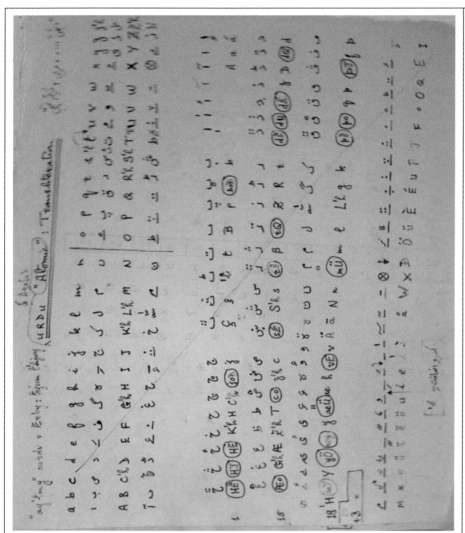

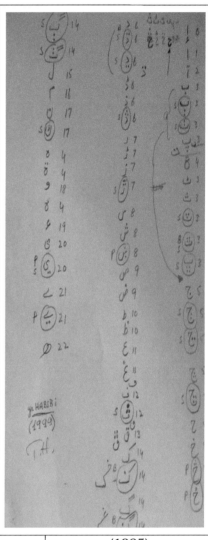

(2019)

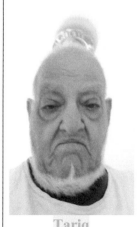

Tariq

European Atomic Alphabet ... 13*4=52 (a pack of cards)

a b c d e f g h i j k l m * n o p q r s t u v w x y z

A B C D E F G H I J K L M * N O P Q R S T U V W X Y Z

ä ç é è ê ë ï ö ü   Ä Ç É È Ê Ë Ï Ö Ü (French)

à á á ã å æ ì ì î ð ñ ò ó ô õ ø ß ù ú ú û ý ÿ þ

À Á Á Ã Å Æ Ì Ì Î Ð Ñ Ò Ó Ô Õ Ø ß Ù Ú Ú Û Ý Ÿ Þ

etcetera

Arabic

(1985)

Hameed

1960

elle

avait

17

ans

Puis … Tout Frais du Pakistan :
je me suis trouvé à Londres
et j'ai posé une demande
pour Concours de
l'Harmonica à
Straßbourg
en 1963
…
Tariq Hameed … **Personal** History

… Nicole-Jordy.wpl : Championne de Monde d'Harmonica …

… 1965 : Delft Hollande : **Accordion Times**-00-   -88- …

Dedicated to Nicole … of forty-eight years of friendship … we always disputed with each other„ but I we felt and insisted **that** we knew but each other since a half of a century … where she always corrected me; 'minus something' … **that** 'minus something' has materialised now to 'minus two', for the two of us„ since 2010: 'n not 2„ **she being the 'minus'**, unfortunately.

And I always Hoped and Promised her, **that** we will Laugh full **that** day, when the Half became the Full … but it didn't, so my Promise was *Broke*„ for **none**'s fault of mine's or hers … only let's say, I was well Punished; for I *Broke* her Heart: **and to this day, I** Suffer; for how could an **empty** Promise come to be fulfilled: **things** *Broken* **have** never **an end**, 'Cause **Ends** 'Tis-selves can't Never Mend 'Tis-self! Thus is the Eternal Law of **Nature** …
… **How**? Explain me **that**! **Nothing now can ever** Change, as all **Ends**? **Well or Well Not**„ 'n that's that …

Ada Massaro ... **Pittrice** Italiana ... **Nata a Lecce 1949,**

poì a **Roma** ... e Svizzera, Neunburg ... **Personal** History

Ada e Tariq : a la sua Casa, Roma, 2010 ...

Denise : sua figlia e mia Tina, Roma ... 1985 ...

Painting in my Personal Possession ... My Italian Sis ...

My German **Grand-Mother** ... (Germany/Deutschland "Offenburg") ... Meine Deutsche **Gross-Mutter**

... Tariq Hameed and **Renate** Geppert ... **Meine Deutsche Gross-Mutter** ... in der Nähe von **Schwartzwald** ...
Madre/Mutter Theressa (India) ... **Thrice** she went & **Helped** her ... **Dreimal** ging sie und **Half** ihr!

… My Tina: most Brainy doggy I ever saw … I spoke to her in **7** Languages … She Obeyed Instantly … Stunned on my Stand? How DARE a Fly Invades OUR Privacy … **Planning** a way, **to** Jump **to** Destroy …

… A Part of my Personal Life **…** **1. MA** English (**Hon urs Pak**) **2.** Chartered Accountant (**UK**) **3.** IT Consultant (Invented World 1st. Accounting Package, on Punch Cards in 1970: **France**) **4.** IT **Miracle** (Invented World 1st. Chemical Data-Base, Punch Cards in 1972-74: **Basel-Swiss**) **5.** Linguist & Poet (**4 L**anguages) **6.** Atomic Alphabet (**Arab**) **7.** Auto **Qur'aan** (**Translation**)

Tariq Hameed standing on his Basel Switzerland Herbstmesse Stand … International Handicrafts Fair … in 20 years of Fairs … I had the **Hon ur** of Meeting Folks about 20 Million!

... **Handicrafts**: Pakistan, India & Thailand ... Main Items were **Carpets**, Clothes, Decor, Silk Scarfs, Ties, Jewelry ... Thus my main Clients being **W**omen, I came to have a good **Insight into L**adies Minds & **Problems: of Mother, Wife & Sis & Daughter** ... Met Millions in **7** **L**anguages ...

... A Part of my Personal Life ... **1.** **MA** English (**Hon**o**urs** **Pak**) **2.** Chartered Accountant (**UK**) **3.** IT Consultant (Invented World 1st. Accounting Package, on Punch Cards in 1970: **France**) **4.** IT **Mira**c**le** (Invented World 1st. Chemical Data-Base, Punch Cards in 1972-74: **Basel-Swiss**) **5.** Linguist & Poet (**4** **L**anguages) **6.** Atomic Alphabet (**Arab**) **7.** Auto **Qur'aan** (**Translation**)

... Obrist resembled so much my **Papa** in Looks & **Mind**, that I Started calling him **Papa** ... We were always together going Sighting Eating in his car, that All *Basel* named him also **Papa** ... in he was , then shifted with **Son** to another Town ... **'Twas the Last that I saw him!**

Tariq Hameed ... **Personality** **Signature Analysis**   (Deutschland Hannover 1993)

1. *Upper & Lower **Loops***

1.1. **Intelligence**: Even height & depth shows a person acting **intuitively**, with no compelling reason to think analytically, preferring to rely on internal feelings and unexplained intuitions ... as "raison d'être" of Active 'n Acting Reason.

1.2. **Emotions**: Thus following an accordance with the intimate **Thoughts**, making no great demands on Life; *content with the own self and all that's around.*

2. *Spacing Characteristics*

2.1. **Will-P**ower: Density shows eagerness to try all out in full innocence; resolutely with enthusiasm, trying to **complete tasks even less pleasant**.

2.2. **Character**: **Optimistic**, enjoying daily aspects of Life; the *cheerful and vivacious* manner enabling to **solve** even most **difficult problems** in an original **way**.

3. *Breadth & Style Formations*

3.1. **Communication**: Ability, of a very **approachable** attitude; talkative without any indiscretion & able to *keep all told secrets, securely in confidence.*

3.2. **V**itality: **Challenges attacked without hes**itation: *exerting strength & **mastering problems by a fresh & lively method***, as energy lasts; but making last surely.

Scope Analysis   (Left Palm Image)

4. *Internal & Personal Matters*

4.1. **Character**: U may work far from home, experiencing many changes in Life & **working quite late old**; sharp & capable, **good planner** *who works out simple solutions to complicated problems.* This talent which few people possess, when properly cultivated, enables U to **make new & effective discoveries**.

4.2. Love **& Marriage**: Quarrels can arise timely during courtship, due to your strong will & habits. *Quite a few disappointments in love affairs will come*, taking a lot of **time for wound healing**. This what exists as from your young age„ may make U miss your chance to marry; but U may well succeed **Late to Mate**.

5. *External & Worldly Matters*

5.1. **Career & Money**: Your **family background made U mature early**, enjoying a comfortable Life young. U dilly-dally & slack of old, risking so to squander early fortune; don't procrastinate, work harder to have NOT regrets older. Eager to succeed, your ***anxiety can lead U to fail***, that may not even ends meet; so be patient & slow down: to GAIN by acting prematurely NOT.

5.2.   Health: Quite healthy & energetic, **U care for yourself**. Be not over confident, as minor ailments ignored, can do harm: *if giddy, check blood pressure.*

6. *General Advice*

6.1.   **To Know What & How to do is Good** : But **When to do is better**. <u>Act timely</u>; **Wait**?

6.2.   **Being Capable U reason out How to Act** : *Timing* is important: often **the jealous**
... may **feel** too well, that probably, may U like it or not ...
that ... *your high performance, is designed to vaunt to belittle others.*

Character Analysis (<u>of 2012</u>) ... Tolerance to Routine

- **Style**: Supple and Accepting ... In a Global manner, you live a Life, **organised and well structured**: not tending to bow to Newness and Variety, at any price; only Leaning to Necessity, **if Reason Be**! You are at Ease, in your mundane habits and manners ...
  your Past 'n your, Present in One Self ... in special, for your Future 'n a Better-Half Self!
- Fundamentally, you need to dedicate yourself to a person, who professes Righteous and Exclusive Love Terms, mutually. However, your tolerance to feeble phantasies ...
  shows a goodness 'n a Greatness of your Heart 'n your Soul: a sole goal role!
- You **disdain** the Concept of **Oscillating Engagements**, **or** of **Total Liberty**; this is what goes against your Concept of the <u>Purity of Sentiments</u> ...
  You desire sharing the "**Good 'n Bad**" moments, **in common 'n in calm!**
- Even if you like to maintain a permanent liaison with your natal family, but it precludes not, that you blab-out all to all 'n every: so you maintain a **reasoned balance** ...
  balancing your **Self**: 'tween **your own 'n your else!**
- Your Elderly **Style** is "**Democratic**": so certain connivance and a true Effective Proximity, in all your Relationships; be it towards the Superiors or Inferiors. That, the **limits be considered limits** true, of structured rapports, 'tween Equals 'n Similar: constructing ...
  a **harmonious 'n so stable a union**, as practical as possible!
- In your opinion, a **balanced Education**, as **well for** Elders, as **well for Juniors**, rigorous 'n effective, *leaving Structural Betterment for both*, is the Call of the Day ...
  a simple **Call to Comfort, generating Traces of** Stability **and of** Elegance!
- Etymologically speaking, Masks are the Essentials of your Life ... the Notion of the Mask, dates from the Old Ages„ the Three **Gongs** of **Destiny** of the **T**heatres of Antiquity; 'n of Masks of Argil, ably borne by Actors of Yester-Days? "Life **is a tale, told by an Idiot**" ... of Masks ... 'n **Above** of **BeYond** !
  Masks which **Hide** 'n Masks which Reveal, which **'n** which of <u>Truths</u>„ 'n which **Falsity** of Life!
- Your Personality is the **Hidden** Story„ be Revealed or Un- Revealed, to these **Strangers** called "**Men**". Thus, our **Being** is Touched by What is Open 'n What is **C**losed: these Variations of Comportment, our Real 'n True <u>Inner-Self</u>„ a Time often which Cries; 'n Times some which **Laugh** ... so ...

Soul-less or full; Suffers or Beatifies our Cores 'n our Corpses ... what so Constitutes our Mental?

BE OR NOT ... Be?   **Where's the Q**uestion?   (**B**oolean **Mathematics**)

... Red ... Atomic Digit Letters ... Super-Imposed Diacritics ... Multiply Posed Image Elements ...

(Animation) http://www.noor-us-samaawat.com/#A1&5.1. (Slide Bar ... Next)

دوذ و دوزخ، دوذ و دوزخ؛ سَرم تم کو اَبھی نَئیں آتی :

کعبہ کی سمت ہے کیا؟ یاں یا واں یا کاں ؟ بر نَئیں آتی!

اَور جب تھا قَدَم طارق کا، دِہلیز باہر واَندر میں؛

تو سَدّاد و غَدّار کیا؟ کیا عاقبت بھی دُکھ نَئیں آتی ؟

... "اَبجَد اُردُو بر قُرآنی طَرز" ... مُکَمَّل ... {۲۰۱۸/۱۰/۲۹}

... یوں جیسے دَستی کِتابَت ... ۱ ... ح ... د ... ر ... س ... ع ... نُجّٰہ عَلیحدہ ...

۱ ... ب ... (ق) ... خ ... ذ ... ن ... س ... ض ... ظ ... غ ... ن ... و ... ئ ... ی ... (ے) ... صّلے.

.1.
Under in Hell,
Over is Hell;
Ashamed are you Not:

.2.
Which Way Lies Prayer?
Here, There, Where?
Ashamed but you'r Not!

.3.
And When,
Puts a Foot down Tariq,
In 'n Out Door-step unto:

.4.
Then Who Low is
or Traitor is?
Ashamed of Thine
Fate, are Thee Not?

(Animation) http://www.noor-us-samaawat.com/#A1&5.1. (Slide Bar ,,, Next)

ہَم کو ہَم کو، نَہ آنا نَہ جَانا، یاں ہی اَست و بَست ؛

نَژول تم کو ہونَائیں یارو: کہ سَب ہیں اَنَخُود میں مَست !

اَور جب تک رَواں رَواں رَہے دُنیا میں طارق ، یوں گَستی میں؛

تو آئیس و عَطَس کیا ہے ہوں ؟ بھا ناروں میں، دَست بہ دَست!

... "اَبجَد اُردُو بر قُرآنی طَرز" ... مُکَمَّل ... {۲۰۱۸/۱۰/۳۱}

... یوں جیسے دَستی کِتابَت ... ح ... د ... ر ... گستی ... س ... نُجّٰہ عَلیحدہ ...

۱ ... ب ... ت ... (ق) ... ٹ ... ح ... خ ... د ... ذ ... ر ... ن ... س ... ص ... ض ... ط ... ظ ... ع ... غ ... ن ... و ... ف ... ئ ... ی ... (ے) ... صّلے.

.1.
We 'n All Us We,
Neither Come Nor Go;
Here's Our Be Or Is;

.2.
Friends you're but
in No-Where, Any-Where?
As in In-Self, is is Is!

.3.
And When,
Floats a World Tariq,
Sail Ships Sad Seas unto:

.4.
Flairing a Fire 'n or
Thirst What Is?
A Floating **Flame,**
Desolate in Desolate Is?

THINKS 'n THOUGHTS

'tween nine 'n fifteen

B|c-o|k   01 **LIVRE   01**

My Father *Died*, on

the 16th. of January 1957 (Lahore)

It was the 9th. Birthday of my Brother ... *who*

Innocently Clapped Hands and Asked for his Present ?

He got none ! (. . . *Then I* stopped *writing ... till 1966 ...*)

= =

tayles 'tween struts 'n frets ... 1 ... **THINKS 'n THOUGHTS**

B◼◼k 05a   1992 **Volume**   Themes   **IV**

...

tayles 'tween struts 'n frets ... 2   THINKS 'n THOUGHTS

B**oo**k   05b   1993 **Volume**   Themes   **IV**

...

tayles 'tween struts 'n frets ... 3 THINKS 'n THOUGHTS

B**o**ok   05c   1993 Volume   Themes   IV

B o o k 02 LIVRE 02 -3--92-

B o o k 04 LIVRE 04 1-32--121-

B o o k 06 LIVRE 06 -1--55--144-

Penser sur Pensées PENSER sur PENSÉES

CONTENTS   BOOK 3   French & English   Volume 1/2

INDEX   THINKS 'n THOUGHTS   1974 ===> 1987   PENSER sur PENSÉES

Per vedere l'Originale (For the Original of) Kublai Khan ... **-10--115** & **-11--115**

Kublai Khan (talvolta scritto Kubla Khan) e il suo impero provocarono folli voli di fantasia tra gli Europei dal tempo della spedizione di Marco Polo del 1271-1292. Ma chi era il Gran Khan, davvero? Una visione romantica del regno di Kublai Khan giunse al poeta inglese Samuel Taylor Coleridge in un sogno intriso di oppio, ispirato dalla lettura del racconto di un viaggiatore britannico e descrivendo la città come Xanadu. S.T. Coleridge, *Kubla Khan*, 1797

...................................Stanza 1

1.

In Xanadu il Kubla Khan

Un magnifico plazzo con duomo decreta:
Dove **Alph**, fiume d'aqua sacra, in mezzo del camin
Dove i uomoni passano i caverni sensa dimension
Andando a un mare sensa sole laciando ogni speranza.

6.

Due volte cinque miglia di terra fertile ronde
I muri e torri cinti in rotond:
E c'erano giardini luminosi di sinuosi ruscelli,
Dove sbocciarono l'incenso dei alberi tanti;
E dove fiorirono le foreste e colline antiche,
Avvolgendo le macchie di soleggiante verde.

...................................Stanza 2

12.

Ma oh! quale profondo baratro romantico obliquo
Traversando la verde collina sotto copertura di cedro!
Un luogo selvaggio di fate! santo e incantato
Sempre sotto come una luna ossessionata calante
Come una donna piangendo per il suo demone-amante!

17.

E da questo baratro, con incessante tumulto ribollente,
Come se la terra in sorsi veloci e densi era respirante,
Una potente fontana fu brevemente forzata:
Mezzo al cui il rapido scoppio era interrotto a metà
Volteggiavano grandine rimbalzante enormi frammenti,
E sotto il flagello-trebbiatrice di pula, cadeva i granelli:
Che in mezzo a queste rocce danzanti allo stesso tempo
Dunque alzò in un attimo le onde del fiume sacro.

25.
Cinque miglia serpeggianti con un movimento intricato
Attraverso boschi e valli scorreva il fiume sacro,
Poi raggiunse le caverne incommensurabili per l'uomo,
E affondò in tumulto in un oceano senza vita:
E' in mezzo-tumulto che ha sentito da lontano Kubla
                    Voci ancestrali profetizzano la guera!

31.
Nel ombra della cupola dei piaceri
Galleggiava a metà tra le onde;
Dove si udì la mista misura
Dalla fontana alle grotte.
È stato un miracolo di dispositivo raro,
Puro piacere, cupola soleggiata con grotte di ghiaccio!

....Stanza 3

37.
Una damigela con un dulcimer
Una visione una sola volta che ho visto;
Era una abissina signiorina,
E sul suo dulcimer ha suonato,
Il Canto del Monte Abora.

42.
Potrei ristabilire dentro di me
La sua sinfonia del suo canto,
Un piacere così profondo mi avrà conquistato,
Che come musica forte e lunga,
Costruirei quella cupola ariosa nell'aria,
Quella cupola solare! quelle grotte di ghiaccio!

48.
E tutti che hanno sentito dovrebbero vederli li,
E che tutti piangenno, Attenzione! Attenzione!
I suoi occhi lampeggianti, e i capelli fluttuanti!
A lui intrecci un cerchio intorno volte tre,
Poi chiudi gli occhi con santo terrore,
Poiché di rugiada di miele si è nutrito,
E bevuto il latte del Paradiso.
54.

A GRAMMATICAL MIRACLE

567 Words ... **A Single Phrase** ... **No** Punctuation Mark

41. (Vaticano) S W A L L O W S *no punctuation* Visions-3- 1993 Original-**thBk-E-5b** 30 باب

a swarm **of**
swallows behind a **swarm** of *swallows* and
when you turned the **other** **way** round another **swarm**
of *swallows* **rapidly** **changing** itself into a different **swarm**
of *swallows* **which** rose up in the sky like smoke with veils in *front*
and veils in the back when they turn and squirm and float *like*
one body and a unique serpentine body going up and *down*
and side to side then turning and returning becoming thicker *and*
thinner and even more thinner than thin and suddenly transforming
back to thicker and thicker when they turn to return to the point where
they started to end not but to continue their play their game playing in
hordes of happiness of individual but united units of thousands of
differences so exceptionally knit together in harmony that only words
and mere words lacked to describe them as you see them and hear them
and feel them in their multiple beauty but such a multiple beauty that
could be pointed out in every individual *swallow* which followed *its*
own individual path and its own individual destiny but at the *same*
instant become part of a screen of smoke of a big swarm **of**
swallows which twisted and turned in thicker **and thinner veils and veins**
of smoky squirling columns against a **totally poised grey sky in all**
intertranspercing to mingle separate
destinies into a common destiny
permitting to exist not lone
or lonely but as a
compact mass
sometimes
massive
some
time

sparse

but always fluidly

flowing dissolving itself slowly

and very steadily from your mind and your

eye to keep on flying and flying away and away always

fainter and fainter but always present and existing but fading

and fading in spite of your most desperate efforts to follow them **with**

your minding eye further and further away against a grey sky and so very **far**

that you were obliged to voyage in time and space and become still so another **person**

in a different spot and different hour who followed with a real and true curious eye a **swarm**

of *swallows* after a *swarm* of *swallows* which steadily and quietly without noise or **sound**

will slowly again start to disappear going further and further away sometimes so **thick**

but sometimes thin and sometimes up and sometimes diving down for the pleasure

of a third person and a third vision which will follow them for a short moment

these *swarms* of *swarms* of *swallows* silently sliding in the sombre skies

knowing well in his inner mind that this swarm of swallows **will continue eternally**

as far and as long as they live without separations **without divisions nor any**

showy sort of punctuations nor stops followed by your **mindful eye flying**

just on and on keeping themselves afloat in the

balancing airs unrelentlessly on without

ever any rests or stops or even a

single comma any smallest

pause or or even any

slight disturbance

existing sole on their

softy movements only

'n so seemingly thus as

pointless reasons of flying

and of flowing disappearing

gradually dissolving far away

and without a point and even a

very and a very small **half stop and I**

say it too by such simple **words of mouth**

without pauses or commas or

any points   of rest just

flying and   high flying

swarms of swarms   of swallows never

never ever coming   to a stop a fullstop

this phenomena observed at **vaticano roma** and confirmed over ka'aba makkah

for birds being very proper creatures mira**culously** hold the clean as flying

you **have** *to* See *the* Sound *the* Sense *the* Sensitive *all* **in a** Single Swap

strangely it is one Sentence **without** a minimum Punctuation Mark

Al-Fil : An Ancient Story   **of the Owners of the Elephants**

https://www.publicdomainpictures.net/en/hledej.php?hleda=swallow ... clipart-vogel-schwalbe-illustration ...
https://www.publicdomainpictures.net/fr/hledej.php?hleda=%C3%A9l%C3%A9phant
... elephant-sunset-painting-vintage ... elephant-sunset-silhouette-1525499048ISC ...

I N D E X ...

Al-Fateha Atomised … See Eiffel-Tower

ح = خ ْ : خ = د ُ : ذ = د ِ : ز = ن ْ : ن = ط ْ : ط = ظ : ص ْ : ص = ض ْ : ض = غ : غ ْ : غ = ق ْ : ق = ب : ت ْ : ت = ث : س ْ : س = ش : و ُ = ؤ

ال لّٰ ه

ال لّٰ ه   لِ لّٰ ه

الــلّٰ ةَ   الــلّٰ هُ

ب ِس ْم ِ   ال لّٰ ه ِ

ال رَّح ْمٰن ِ   ال رَّح ِى ْم ِ

اَل ْح َم ْد ُ   لِ لّٰ ه ِ

رَبِّ ال ْع ٰل َم ِى ْن َ

ال رَّح ْمٰن ِ   ال رَّح ِى ْم ِ

م ٰلِك ِ ى َو ْم ِ ال دّ ِى ْن ِ

اِیَّاك َ ن َع ْب ُد ُ و َاِیَّاك َ ن َس ْت َع ِى ْن ُ

اِه ْد ِن َا ال صّ ِرَاط َ ال ْم ُس ْت َق ِى ْم َ ﴿g001﴾

ص ِرَاط َ ال َّذ ِى ْن َ ا َن ْع َم ْت َ ع َل َى ْه ِم ْ

غ َى ْر ِ ال ْم َغ ْض ُو ْب ِ ع َل َى ْه ِم ْ و َل َا ال ضّ آلِّى ْن َ ﴿001غ﴾

ط َار ِق ُ ح َم ِى ْد ُ   ط َار ِق ُ ح َم ِى ْد ُ

DEC 22 1999
9:55:47 PM

-1- -xiv-*I*014.

Prediction

Extra Bright

Full Moon

Occured …

in December

22, 1999

Full
Moon
1901

THE OLD FARMER'S ALMANAC PREDICTS :

This year the full moon will occur on the Winter Solstice (December 22nd) called the first day of Winter. Since the full moon on the Winter Solstice will occur in conjunction with a lunar perigee (point in the moon's orbit that is closest to Earth) The moon will appear about 14% larger than it does at apogee (the point in its elliptical orbit that is farthest from the Earth)   … Since the Earth is also …

several million miles closer to the sun at this time of the year than in the summer, sunlight striking the moon is about 7% stronger making it brighter. Also, this will be the closest perigee of the Moon of the year since the moon's orbit is constantly deforming.

      If weather's Clear and there's snow cover by you,

          it is believed that car headlights will be superfluous.

DEC 22 1999
9:56:19 PM

♪♫ uhu ♪♫ ut B(c-o)k URDU *thBk-Q-01A*66-yrs*.pdf طارق حمیب THINKS 'n THOUGHTS -Ap--01-

-2- -xv-*T*015 Other Tales طارق حمیب ... 23/12/1999 ... i saw this mO-On ...

Full moon at Perigee & at Apogee … A Portuguese amateur astronomer Antônio Cidadão, captured these images of the full Moon on two different dates using a black-and-white QuickCam on a 4-inch f/6.3 Schmidt-Cassegrain telescope. In the left-hand image the Moon was at perigee, i.e., closest to Earth. In the right-hand image it was at apogee, i.e., farthest from Earth. the differences in the Moon's size, are quite ... apparent

SKY & TELESCOPE RESPONSE: **Brightest Moon in 133 Years**?

Per Roger W. Sinnott, associate editor of Sky & Telescope magazine, the answer is an unequivocal: **No**!

It is true that there is a most unusual coincidence of events this year. As S&T contributing editor Fred Schaaf points out in the December 1999 issue of Sky & Telescope, "The Moon reaches its very closest point all year on the morning of December 22nd. That's only a few hours after the December solstice and a few hours before full Moon. Ocean tides will be exceptionally high and low that day." But to have these three events -- lunar perigee, solstice, and full Moon -- occur on nearly the same day is not especially rare. The situation was rather similar in …

December 1991 and December 1980, as the following dates and Universal Times show:

Event	Dec. 1999	Dec. 1991	Dec. 1980
Full Moon	22, 18h	21, 10h	21, 18h
Perigee	22, 11h	22, 9h	19, 5h
Solstice	22, 8h	22, 9h	21, 17h

What really rare is, is that in 1999 the three events take place in such a quick succession. On only two other occasions in modern history have the full Moon, lunar perigee, and December solstice coincided within a 24-hour interval, coming just 23 hours apart in 1991 (as indicated in the preceding table) and 20 hours apart back in 1866. The 10-hour spread on December 22, 1999, is unmatched at any time in the last century and a half.

So is it really true, as numerous faxes and e-mails to Sky & Telescope have claimed that, the Moon will be brighter this December 22nd, than at any time in the last 133 years ? We have researched the actual perigee distances of the Moon throughout the years 1800-2100, and here are some perigees of "record closeness" that also occurred at the time of full Moon:

Century	Date	Distance (km)	Date	Distance (km)
19 th.	1866 Dec. 21	357,289	1893 Dec. 23	356,396
20 th.	1912 Jan. 4	356,375	1930 Jan. 15	356,397
21 st.	1999 Dec. 22	356,654	2052 Dec. 6	356,421

It turns out, then, that the Moon comes closer to Earth in the years 1893, 1912, 1930, and 2052 than it does in either 1866 or 1999. The difference in brightness will be exceedingly slight. But if you want to get technical about it, the full Moon must have been a little brighter in 1893, 1912, and 1930 than in either 1866 or 1999, (based on the calculated distances).

The 1912 event is undoubtedly the real winner, because it happened on the very day the Earth was closest to the Sun that year. However, according to a calculation by a Belgian astronomer Jean Meeus, the full Moon on January 4, 1912, was only 0.24 magnitude (about 25 percent) brighter than an "average" full Moon.

In any case, these are issues only for the Astronomical Record Books. This month's full Moon won't look dramatically brighter than normal. Most people won't notice a thing, despite e-mail chain letters, implying that we'll see something amazing.

Our data is from the U.S. Naval Observatory's ICE computer program, Jean Meeus's Astronomical Algorithms, page 332;

and the August 1981 issue of Sky & Telescope**, page 110.** Question is … Can our OooolllooO-e-aaaAMMMAaaa Calculate so 222

<u>Nota</u> : Date of a Grand Prophet … J. Christ … Before C (in Minus -) … After C (in Plus +) … Christ Ô Christ Ô Christ ? Christianity ? ? ?

Hi Hi … Very Good Mathematicians SIR … Where's the YEAR ZERO 0000 ???? … False Gregorian Cal. by 1 yr … Hi Hi

1.   This year the full moon will occur on the Winter **Solstice** (December 22nd) … named the **First day of Winter**

2.   The full moon on the Winter solstice will occur **in conjunction with a Lunar Perigee** … (point in the moon's orbit that is closest to Earth)

3.   The **moon will appear about 14% larger** than it does at **Apogee** … (point in its elliptical orbit that is farthest from the Earth)

4.   Since the Earth is *also several million miles closer to the sun at this time of the year* … than in summer, **sunlight striking the moon is about 7% stronger making it brighter**

5.   Also, this will be the **closest perigee of the Moon of the year** … since the *moon's orbit is constantly deforming*

6.   If the weather is Clear and there is a snow cover where you live … *it is well believed that* … **car headlights will be superfluous**

Other Facts are … 22nd. December 1999 Full Moon … (Tariq Hameed) طارق حميد

7.   This full moon lay in the **Month of Ramadhan** (Islamic Year) … Astronomy proves … *that Ramadhan generally remains around the middle of year, at the Turn of Century*

8.   Further, history proves that '*Ramdhan*' **seldom** divides itself over the Turn of a Century

9.   However, this time 'twas a Miracle … the Turn of a Millennium … **never to happen again**

10.   *Thus, we can Conclude that* … "Light Will Dawn Again on a Sleeping Civilisation"

11.   *Strangely*, a couple of days later, i.e., the Night of 24-25 December ('*Xmas & Boxing Day*), there was a violent storm in Europe, with Winds flowing at over 170 km p/h, completely destroying the entire Electric System of ALL European Countries … … Only in France, more than 3 million Trees were Up-rooted … & In-spite of Free Govt. Gift, some are still lying around … Abandoned …

12.   As a Result, the wHole of Europe and mƐ-Əst of America **passed in Darkness at 'Xmas**

13.   *It can be Supposed* … that this **Play of Light & Darkness** … have *Hidden Surprises for us*

14.   *Also to be remembered,* that Events Occurring on Turn of Centuries, have **long time life span … Examples are a Real Wonder … … to cite a few …**

➢   **1495** AD … **Error** of Christophorus Columbus … *Discovering America*, instead of India

➢   **1565** AD … Siege of Malta : Followed by **Lépante** … *Turks Lost Sea Supremacy for ever*

➢   **1595** AD … Elisabeth I & **Shakespeare** … *Begins British Empire* : **English** Domination

➢   **1699** AD … **January 26** : Treaty of Karlowitz (Turkey & Venice, Poland, Austria) … *Turks quit C-Europe*

➢   **1795** AD … The **French Revolution** … Base of the *Modern Republics* and *Democracy*

➢   **1895** AD … The Planetary **Industrial Revolution** … Colonialism falls into a Death Phase

➢   **1995** AD … Starts an '**Age of Illumination**' … *Justice to Prevail* … **IF** Humans want to Survive

'Twas my main Reason … *in Advance I Knew* … a Dominant Event of FUTURE.

The Rise of a LOST Civilisation … I SAW this mƟ-Ɵn … & I Knew What I had TO DO. NᵒᵒRᵉus▸ Samᵃᵃ waT

… Thus I Launched this Struggle to **Establish Urdu in Pakistan**, starting with Computer ID Cards …

… There was Dr. Chaudri (Patron) : TH (Brains) … Habibullah, Saeed Ahmed, Imran Qureshi (*& Action*) …

If Only 5 Dedicated Persons can **Change** a **Destiny**, a **Future** : So, Let's **ALL** but **Together** … **Wake UP** Humanity?

الْمَلَٰٓئِكَةِ. .كا. .سَفَرٌ.

▲

▲

▲I-I ▲ I-I▲

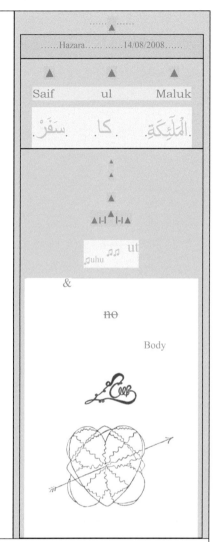

uhu ut

&

~~no~~

Body

...نَقْشْ...فَرْيَادِیْ ...هَےْ ...اللّٰهِ... ... Visible ... be ... ▲I-I ▲ I-I▲

... Visible...soit... ▲I-I ▲ I-I▲.........▲I-I ▲ I-I▲...immer...ist...
...
...Traversée...des... ▲ nges...... ▲ ngels...here...Toe-Tip...

t h u q k y @ g m a i l . c o m

t h o o k y @ g m a i l . c o m

Queen Victoria Learning Urdu With her Tutor Ustad Abdul Karim

© 2002 T. Hameed   Page 2 of 28   29/06/1999

اُردُو کی تَرقّی کی لیے
مُقتَدِرہ قَومی زُبان (پسپور)
پشاور اور تھرپارکر (تھرپارکر)
سمیت ٹیکناوجی کے نئے
راستوں کا تَعیُّن کر رہا ہے

اُردُو کی تَرقّی کی لیے
مُقتَدِرہ قَومی زُبان
(پسپور) پشاور اور
تھرپارکر (تھرپارکر)
سمیت ٹیکناوجی کے نئے
راستوں کا تَعیُّن

رَمْ	:	تَیْ
وّ	:	قُ
پَ	:	پَ
تُھٔ	:	تھ
بِ	:	تِ
دُ	:	ٹُ
حِ	:	جِ
دِ	:	ک

Font … Digital Numeric Atomic **Urdu-Arabic** … Quick-Zohar Tariq Hameed Created طارق حمید

١. بے زیست رہا اس فاٸی فناء مِیں … بسا بس نورِ السَّمٰوات بعد:

٢. جہاں جہاں ھمیں اور کھیں ھمیں !

ہے تو صرف، بعد آباد ؛ بعد کے بعد !

٣. اور جب ہاتھ ہلا الوداع لیے طارِق ، دنیا کو دنیا مِیں ؟

٤. ھمیش 'آدھا' رہا ! 'سارا' بس بن نہ سکا … ہزارہا کاوشوں کے بعد ؟

.1. **Without** Existence was I, in this **Fake World** …
Living only in a **Cosmos beYond** … 'n **After!**

.2. Where There IS No**Where** … a No**Where** of **Nothing!**
If There **IS**, then **IS** an After; After the **After!**

.3. **And When,** shaking Hands bye-bye
says Tariq, to this **World**, in this **World unto?**

.4. Ever remains BUT a '**HALF**'! **N**ever a **Being** '**FULL**' …
Thousands 'n Thousand of **Pains After?**

STS

N T C :   National Translation Center

We have now available, the top-most expertise of National and International standing and repute, in the all fields relating to Translatology.

➤ Provide a "High-End" Languages Conversion Service
➤ Analyze carefully thus, the basic Urdu Elements:
    ❖ the text and context flow of the primary data
    ❖ the terminological and technical matter content
➤ Determine so, the underlying rules of Urdu Computer Grammar
➤ Launch a Multi-National level Urdu Editor (all functionalities)
➤ Develop scientifically an Automatic Translation System : ATS
    (Machine Translation, popularly named MT)

This is a pious and demanding, but a long-term project, almost in the realm of fantasy; however, we are confident of our goal, as each one of our collaborators is a master of many tongues and crafts.

Confidentiality

Is our keyword! Working in coordination with top-class lawyers and advocates, we assure our clients of an absolute security guarantee, on their data, on their files; and all other relative information, them concerning.

Usage: A Managerial Tool

We construct our Analysis
    ➤ on Total Reliability
    ➤ on large-scale Data WareHouse Dimensioning
    ➤ on "High-End" Managerial Convenience (not operator dominated)

Methodology

Moving Data, from Paper to Computer, is the crying need of the day.
Thus, our systems are designed for 100% accuracy.

Our elder, M.A. (English), F.C.A. (London), Computer Expert, accepts NO Errors!

He Conceived and Implemented the World's 1ˢᵗ Chemical Database
Stable Colors were developed on it; for Mercedez, Parche (and Pakistani Carpets)
    ❖ BORD: Basic Operational Research Data   (CIBA, Switzerland: 1972)
    ❖ Innovation: Multi-Relational, Partial Lockings, Automatized Queryings

This was just short words. Now, Let us have a longer talk.

CHAIRMAN
Dr. Azam Chaudary

CHIEF EXECUTIVE:
Tariq Hameed

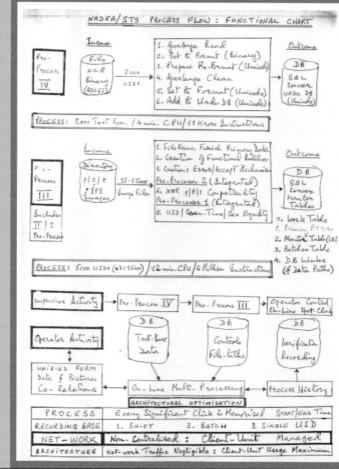

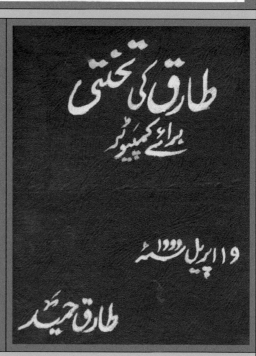

The Honorable Chief Executive

of Our Beloved Country

Respected Sir,

Probably my advice is uncalled for, but I would certainly like to bring up a few points:

1. **Transparence**

The "open declaration" of your tax returns is really commendable. In the betterment of the country, it is a valuable future reference.

Even before, this was a mandatory requirement for politicians in power. Unfortunately, it has never been totally implemented.

In your interest and that of the country, please make this action obligatory in realistic terms. I suggest the following:

➢ The five top grades of the country (in the administrative sense), either nominated or elected on the national or provincial level, should submit this open tax declaration compulsorily; preferably published in the Official Gazette.

➢ This declaration should be yearly. An assets variation (specially Incremental), must be likewise attached along with.

2. **Corruption Roots**

➢ Lack of "Action Transparency"   (British Bureaucracy Legacy)
But then the "Control" was Central   (Kingship)

➢ Limited number of persons   (in Cartel Formations)
Smaller the group, more is it bribable   (Lesser Bribe Costs)

In mutual interest of yourself and the country, any type of future parliamentary or decisionary authority, should have much wider and deeper roots, both in national and provincial constitutions. They would consequently be more numerous and samely more difficult to corrupt, because more costly.

3. **Khushamdees**

Please Be-Aware of "**High-Level**" Pension-Seekers …

History has always proved, that a Well-Intentioned Leader oft is a Prey to the Personal Self Interest "Professional Prætor".

What I call a "Courtier-Clique" now well active in your person are the "Hang-Over" of Older Time: Scrap & Scrub History!

4. **Addendum**

If you think that a change of the Cultural Environment, as for example, especially bringing-up our Traditional Language as a Tool, Powerful & Workable … can be helpful … on the National & the International Scene, I have some Innovative Methodology & Technology, to expose to your Perusal!

With these few Words,

Your Respected Sir,

I remain truly,

'n Loyally A Private Citizen.

Tariq Hameed : 29/10/1999

thooky@gmail.com

5. **Homage to Pak Post**

For over 6 months, **Gen Agha** Cordially Invited me to Lodge in his Own Office as DG …

Day & Night I Worked on Urdu & **Qura'an** Digital Atomisation! "All my Immense Thanks, for a Great Service to the Nation".

General of only 17 ... Tariq-bin-Ziad ... who gave his Name to Gibraltar! طارق حميد

'Tis was a Calm 'n Quiet Eve: three ships folded their Sails 'n glided softly to a stop,, as the Sun Set Sweetly 'n called it a day ... on such a Settling Night! That Night he knew ... that who Controls "Gibl-ut-Tariq", Controls the World! **Rocky Mount of** Tariq, thus made History: forever,, as a few Sea-Gulls, headed at ease, Sky-High to their Niches.

In a previous plan, Tariq had already gaged the Spaniard Despotic Usurper Rodrigues' Strength and Weaknesses ... so this time, in 711 he was fully prepared ... he had but a meagre 7000 men against an Armoured Cavalry, esteemed about over 70.000,, thus he had to Plan otherwise: a Clever Tactic, that left not even a suspicion of Defeat!

The night was young 'n Stars Sparkled ... Tariq moved his men to Inner Fortifications ... then in the Calm Sea, at Dawn-break, rose Flames 'n Fire; thus in a matter of minutes, all Ships existed No More; remained Ashes 'n Smoke: No Sails, No Rams, No Planks ... just Ghost Silhouettes of Past Grandeur, Sunk in Waters 'n Waves! Tariq had got up early in the Golden Morn with a few Courageous Friends ... 'n had put ALL to Fire ... **A Path of No Return**!

Then he Spoke: "**F**riends, **F**aithful 'n **F**ighters,, **E**vil **L**ives **S**hort, but **G**lory **L**ives **E**ternally! Ô, you People of Belief, where is the Escape? Behind's the Sea 'n Cert Death: but afore you, is Probable Death but Cert Glory,, **DO or DIE**? ▲ı-ı▲ı-ı▲ (God) is with you ... and all you Need,, is **Nothing** but **Perseverance 'n Confidence 'n Patience 'n Faith**"!

19th. July, 711 AD, at Wadi-Bakkah (Salado): the demoralized Rodrigues' Army,, immediately shed in blood, was put to flight ... however, Tariq did not Laud his success, but swiftly chased them, for he had realised that the Armoured over-loaded **Goth** Cavalry, was No Match for valiant 'n super-speeding horse-men, lightly clad to manoeuvre swift!

Now a few Words about ... the **Boat-Burning Tradition** ... It has existed, 'n was practiced even since Antiquity:

1. Classical figures are believed to destroy ships in brave conquest moments: **Alexander**, **Cæsar**, Apostle **Paul**.
2. Giants of **Gog and Magog,** the Great Perm (North Russia) ... turned out to be a Viking Norse (**Boat Funerals**).
3. This **Gog and Magog** Tradition, carries on in Modern Times (**India**) ... Man, Wife, Belongings (**Sati Funerals**).
4. **Portuguese 'n Spaniards**, Hernán Cortés (Yucatan Peninsula: **1519**) ... expansion activities (**Trading Rituals**).

Rodrigues drowned in River Salado ... 'n thus Tariq carried on, his soldiers inspired by his very able Promptness: by the end of 711,, Tariq with his Generals had conquered Cordova up-to Toledo (Gothic Capital),, 'n half Spain ... However, Tariq's Superior, Musa bin Nusair, thinking that Tariq's Forces may-be out-numbered, ordered him not to expand any more: but Tariq, knowing these actual Terrains much better, did not obey; as giving a breath-take to the Enemy, could have been Mortal. So Tariq continued, employing his minimum resources to a maximum advantage!

Musa bin Nusair, highly surprised by the phenomenal successes of Tariq, simultaneously landed in Spain with his supporting army ... however, at first, he was truly displeased by Tariq's dis-obedience,, but seeing the true ground Realities, forgave him magnanimously: **to carry on the Spanish Conquest**! After dominating Savilla, he joined Tariq in Toledo,, to carry on to the high-lands of Leon, Aragon and Galicia. Consequently, in only under two years, the two Muslim Veterans, had brought most of Northern Spain, up till the Pyrenees, under their authority!

Musa received peremptory orders of the Caliph Walid, that with his Lieutenant Tariq, they present themselves in Damascus,, where, on their arrival in the Umayyed Capital, in Feb 715, were received with due decorum 'n honour, as Heroes deserve! Unfortunately, the Caliph died soon after: replaced by his brother Suleman, **resentful 'n jealous of their success**! Historians say, that the two Glorious Generals were Humiliated and Dis-Honoured,, to be left on the Streets, in Need 'n in Want ... 'n so is How they Perished ... **for Services Rendered to the Meaner of the Mean**!

The **Mean Never** ... but **the Great Always Leave a Name in History**!

General of only 17 … Tariq-bin-Ziad … who gave his Name to Gibraltar! طارق حميد

Origins of Tariq … was he a Berber,, was he a Moroccan,, was he an Arab … None seems to know? What one knows is that **he was**: with a Name from the **Qura'an** … 'n that's what Counts "**Gibl-ut-**Tariq",, **Boat-Burner**!

Character of Tariq … he possessed an Indomitable Courage,, 'n strong **Will-P**ower,, full Strength 'n Stamina … his Confidence 'n Faith were Infallible,, 'n his Plans were Brilliantly Conceived 'n Harmoniously Executed,, 'n his Military Strategies were Swift 'n Intrepid … He was Mature 'n Self-Disciplined 'n Cool 'n Balanced in Mind, in All 'n Every Adverse or Favourable Circumstances … 'n **Totally a Self-Master**, in Face of the Strongest of Oppositions!

Personality of Tariq … his Fine Personality had many Humanitarian Aspects … Dignified, Self-Restrained, Devout to All 'n his Cause, totally Un-Mindful of **Who** Thought **What** of **What** he did,, but that **Be it Well-Done** … Respectful to his Superiors, Courteous to his Equals 'n Kind 'n Considerate to his Inferiors … One of the very few in History, who have left a **Hall-Mark of Character,, of Intelligence, of Bounty, 'n of Simplicity in Pure Goodness**!

Finally … to Sum Up … **Frailty, Thy Name is W**oman … (Hamlet: Shakespeare)

10,000 Sages Tortured,, mul.mul.Mullaism … Treason,, Thyne Name's Pride … (Me: Shake-a-Pear)

Gibraltar's History … Small Peninsula in Southern Iberia … as Mediterranean Opens …

https://unsplash.com/s/photos/gibraltar
photo-1595353022520-93a6386e0b16.jpg

https://unsplash.com/s/photos/gibraltar
photo-1571081523650-af92f468af65.jpg

History spans over 2,900 years … of reverence in ancient times … to "the most **dense, fortified, contested European Point**".
Gibraltar: populated 50,000 years ago by Neanderthals, ended around 24,000, at their disappearance. After came Phoenicians, Carthaginians, Romans: belief & worship of the **Twin Pillars Hercules Shrines** … **Gibraltar Rock** 'Hollow Rock', *Mons Calpe*!

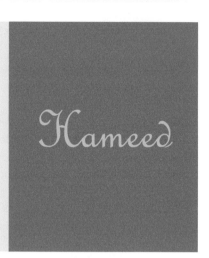

Tariq Hameed

Voracious Reader 'n Searcher, since Two 'n Half years Old, of Where LYES the TRUTH? طارق حمید

"Aye, there Lyes the rub": so in this Hamlet of No Return, called 'World of the Wise Men of Gotham', only but be Bed-Ridden by the Un-Wise of Bottom, my small Wisdom but Swore faintly; "Never Truly Grow-up"!

'Twas Destiny, that born Myopic, Forced me to Imagine. Thus, Truth 'n Purity came to Grasp: it a day dawned that, "Dirt were you Born, to returnest to Dirt" … Empty-Handed Come, 'n Empty-Handed Gone … thus lil by lil, formed a Philosophy: "You only GAIN, what you GIVE" …   Help Humanity; Not your own Self-Self!

Learning thus so early, that Seeing was Un-Truth … Lampions big of Light, Blinking 'n Flickering, so Blown-up in Multi-Fluid Colours in the Deep Depths of the Cosmos' … factually were, Else-Things in the Else-Where? Questions to be Posed 'n Answered: allowing the use of other Senses, like Sounds, Taste, Smell 'n Movements, in Truth to just Re-Construct the feasible Probable Reality; Intuitively analysing the Crayoned cricks 'n cracks of chalky traits, I justly Heard, the Black-Board Talk back to me: 'n Revealed by Magic, the Writing on the Wall … so Un-Veiled, the False-hood of the Persons of Convenience?

Only pictures 'n books were my Mates. Actually, Mental Correction always rectifying the Worldly Vision … suddenly Adult, one put Glasses on my Nose? Help! Ahhhh, the Truth: which I already Knew since so long, by books 'n looks: 'n my Dear Ancient Masters, who had made my Imagination, my Best Friend, for-ever!

Friends ! Live to Give … Fill Graves with Souls, NOT Soles … Tread Down, in Here-After?

Ever Be True: the Mental Remains 'n Captures All as a Pure Child,, never as Sallied Humans: who in Truth are, Not Sapiens, but Serf-Peons! Slaves of the Junky-Jungle-Law: Lead by the Lowly Mi-Lords; by Law?

Sink the Beast, to Save the Sky-Bid Ængels … To be or not to be, that's the Question?

Write 'n Put 25 years in a Drawer. If U find, it still good? It Might have some Value in it … T. S. Eliot.

… TARIQ … ONLY PERSON IN WORLD … WAITING TO PUBLISH TILL 80 … طارق حمید

... **TARIQ** ... ONLY PERSON IN WORLD ... WAITING TO PUBLISH TILL 80 ... طارق حمید

Publishing Planned: 21/02/2021   1st. b**oo**k   **Completion: 05/05/2021**

(Mother's Goodbye-World Anniversary ... '72)   *Kublai Khan*   (Kublai Coronation ... 05/05/1260)

History of **Urdu** … The **Mongol**/Turkish word **Urdu** means "**Camp**" or "**Palace**" ... Kublai ...

… **The Final Place of Rest** … And That's How My Poëm Ends: **S**adly …

*Awaiting; that the L**oo**se **End** Breath, be shed,*
*'N **d**owned he slept: Camp **Urdu** in bed,*
That Spirits to the Ninth Heaven Arise.

That.Spirits.to.the.Ninth.Heaven.Arise   ...   طارق حمید

Beethoven's.9th.Sympohony.first.recording.(Bruno.Seidler-Winkler,1923)

Beethoven's.9th.Sympohony.(Hymn.to.Joy)…https://www.youtube.com/watch?v=nZV2EuA9fwM

Publishing Planned: 16/01/2023   4th. b**oo**k ... 3-2   **Completion: 21/02/2023**

(Father's Goodbye-World ... 16/01/1957)   (73)   *Tayles 'Tween*   (61)   (Ma's Goodbye-World Anniversary ... '72)
Struts 'n Frets ... 2

Publishing Planned: 05/05/2023   5th. b**oo**k ... 3-3   **Completion: 14/08/2023**

(Kublai Coronation ... 05/05/1260)   *Tayles 'Tween*   (Pak Independence (75) ... 14/08/1947)
Struts 'n Frets ... 3

An **Emperor**, Leaning on Staff of his Wealth:

Humiliated, Us Poor Souls' **Love**, by Stealth?

Taj Mahal : Akbar Allahbadi : اکبر الهٰبادی

https://www.pexels.com/photo/black-and-white-photo-of-the-taj-mahal-7582485/

اك شہنشاہ نے دولت

کا سہارا لے کر:

ہم غریبوں کی محبت

کا اڑایا ہے مزاق ؟

Printed in the United States
by Baker & Taylor Publisher Services